LESBIANS TALK

Cherry Smyth

Scarlet Press

❛ Queer:
1. Strange, odd, eccentric; of questionable character, shady, suspect; out of sorts, giddy, faint (feel queer); drunk; homosexual (esp. of man); in Q- street, in difficulty, debt, disrepute
2. Homosexual
3. Spoil, put out of order ❜
'Concise Oxford English Dictionary'

❛ 1. Drunk – Properly, not in your normal state of health, and still rarely used of a drunkard, with a suggestion that condition caused by something else.
"Queered in the drinking of a penny pot of malmsey."
(Walter Scott: 1822 The Fortune of Nigel)
2. Of unsound mind – 'queer in the head' – a bit queer.
3. Homosexual: Almost always of males and equally common as an adjective: "I'm not, um, queer. Well, you know, I don't like boys..." (Theroux: 1975 The Great Railway Bazaar)
Queerdom is a tendency towards homosexuality. ❜
'The Faber Dictionary of Euphemisms', Faber 1989

❧ *In every human being a vacillation from one sex to the other takes place, and often it is only the clothes that keep the male or female likeness, while underneath the sex is the very opposite of what it is above.* ❧ Virginia Woolf, 'Orlando', 1928

❧ *A woman who loves a woman is forever young. The mentor and the student feed off each other.* ❧
Anne Sexton, 'Rapunzel', 1971

❧ *And I would wonder if I were not something else entirely, a man in a woman's body, perhaps, a redneck man in a woman's body, or maybe something even worse – a man who liked to fuck men in a woman's body; that is, a man in a woman's body who fucked women because that was the closest thing a man who was a woman could come to being a homosexual.*❧
Jane DeLynn, 'Don Juan in the Village', 1990

Acknowledgements

My first thanks must go to the bold women at Scarlet Press who grasped at the idea of a queer issues pamphlet in the first place, and encouraged me to run with it. I am especially indebted to the calm and thorough editing job executed on my first drafts by Belinda Budge and Vicky Wilson.

I would also like to thank all the interviewees who made it possible to begin to define the way queer is currently developing in London, and I regret that the scope of the interviews could not extend to other cities and to queers in Ireland.

Finally, my thanks go to friends who have discussed and argued about queer notions with me and to Inge Blackman, Philip Derbyshire and Paul Burston for comments on the work in progress. None of it would have been possible without the lovers, in particular J.D., S.D. and B.A.D., with whom I have relished being queer.

Lesbians Talk Queer Notions is dedicated to all the quare women in Ireland who stayed. **C.S.**

Scarlet Press would like to thank Sue O'Sullivan for her encouragement and advice in the creation of this series.

Published by Scarlet Press
5 Montague Road, London E8 2HN

British Library Cataloguing-in-Publication Data
A catalogue record for this book is available from the British Library
ISBN 1 85727 025 8

Cover design: Pat Kahn
Typesetting: Kathryn Holliday
Printed in Great Britain

Contents

Contributors

Inge Blackman is a film-maker and writer

Tessa Boffin is a queer dyke cultural activist

Paul Burston is a journalist

Philip Derbyshire works for the Gay London Policing Group

Lola Flash is a photographer and former member of Art Positive

Sue Golding is a philosophy professor and director of Buddies in Bad Times Theater Company in Toronto

Della Grace is a photographer

Derek Jarman is a film-maker, writer, queer artist and activist

Isaac Julien is a film-maker

Roz Kaveney is a writer and book reviewer

Mandy McCartin is a painter

Isling Mack-Nataf is a Buddhist, rock-climbing film-maker

Suzanne Moore is a journalist and writer

Ruth Novaczek is a film-maker

Pratibha Parmar is a film-maker

Lisa Power is the Secretary of the International Lesbian and Gay Association

Spike Pittsberg is a writer and member of Women Against Fundamentalism

Sarah Schulman is a writer and member of ACT UP, New York

Linda Semple is a bookseller

Tori Smith is a member of OutRage

Cherry Smyth is an Irish poet and writer who lives in London

Alison Thomas is an environmental health worker

Simon Watney is a writer and activist

Elizabeth Wilson is a writer

Harriet Wistrich is a member of Justice For Women

❝ *I take risks both in my writing and teaching around sexual representation and believe that women could have less repressed attitudes to their bodies and their desires if there were more spaces to present diverse images and texts. I have tried to open up dialogues about taboo subjects and have written about sex in explicit detail in stories which have been dubbed "lesbian erotica" by some and "dirty porn" by others. It is essential that we do not naively follow censorship demands to "protect" women from explicit material as it may further restrict women's access to information, expression and explorations of our sexuality. I have worked on the filmic representation of women and AIDS and hope that frank discussions and accurate information on sexual practices will counter the risks of infection, illness and ultimately death.* ❞ Cherry Smyth

Queer history

❝ The insistence on "queer" – a term defined against "normal" and generated precisely in the context of terror – has the effect of pointing out a wide field of normalisation, rather than simple tolerance, as the site of violence. ❞
Michael Warner, 'Fear of a Queer Planet'

The language of sexualities informs and transforms the cultural, social, political and historical contexts we inhabit. And no naming has been so vociferously contested in recent years as the word 'queer'. In several cities in the US, queer politics has been constituted in movements such as Queer Nation, while Britain has witnessed the birth of the direct action against homophobia group OutRage, with branches in London and other cities with high gay and lesbian populations such as Manchester. But queer identification exists beyond the membership of campaigning groups and signals a more general dissatisfaction with former lesbian and gay politics. The AIDS epidemic triggered anger, disbelief and a renewed sense of disenfranchisement among younger lesbians and gay men, who saw the meek acceptance of marginalisation as leading to a dangerous complacency within the community and victimisation from without. SILENCE = DEATH became the motto of a new generation who refused to be silenced, not only by government neglect in the face of AIDS, but by new homophobic legislation and a dramatic rise in the incidence of queer-bashing. The cry for safer sex information, research and drugs to fight the AIDS epidemic expanded into a campaign against all homophobic oppression. An urgent sense of mortality inspired the rejection of respectability and discretion.

We feel angry and disgusted, not gay. Using 'queer' is a way of reminding us how we are perceived by the rest of the world. It's a way of telling ourselves we don't have to be witty, charming people who keep our lives marginalised and discreet in the straight world. 'Queer' can be a rough word, but it is also a sly and ironic weapon we can steal from the homophobe's hand and use against him. 'NYQ', January 1992

Lesbians Talk Queer Notions aims to document the emergence of queer politics and self-understanding in Britain, primarily, though not exclusively, from a lesbian/dyke perspective. It invites you to take a selective romp through lesbian and gay history and the development of queer politics from a vantage point which does not claim to be representative, but rather exploratory. It is situated firmly within feminism and queer politics, while expressing ambivalences towards both. Does the new defiant and pro-vocative stance associated with queer politics signal a shift in ideology, or is it the wishful activism of a few white gay men? How is queer incorporating feminist and anti-racist strategies? Is queer as radical as it believes itself to be or simply radical chic? Who are the queer artists?

Queer is criminal

The coining of the word 'homosexual' in 1870 quickly led to the develop-ment of a strict binary homo-hetero opposition which still tyrannises notions of sexual orientation, despite the recognition of its increasing inadequacy to identify and describe sexual practice. The idea that there is only one 'good' sexual orientation, based on a correctly gendered object choice, gave rise to a series of oppositions in which homosexuality was deemed evil, abnormal and decidedly 'other', ie queer.

Homosexuality became a medical problem, a pathology, even a disease; and medical and scientific speculations about homosexuality attempted to establish clear borderlines and labels to draw an impassable border between acceptable and abhorrent behaviour. Elaine Showalter, 'Sexual Anarchy'

Marital hetero-sex was reinforced as normative, with all other sexual lifestyles and practices measured against it. Even today, married monogamy is widely cited as a safer sex method by pontificators such as William Rees-Mogg (*Independent*, 2 December 1991), and is often advocated as the best way to repress 'unhealthy' desires. (The appeal of the BBC's *Portrait of a Marriage* drama, which chronicled Vita Sackville-West and Harold Nicholson's queer wedlock was perhaps wider than intended, in a way not readily surmised.) Parents of gay men and lesbians frequently suggest that they marry to keep up appearances and reap the privileges of heterosexual union while having same-sex affairs on the side.

In 1885 the Labouchère Amendment, which specifically identified and outlawed male homosexual acts, was tacked on to the Criminal Law Amendment Act:

Any male person who, in public or private, commits, or is party to the commission of, or procures or attempts to procure the commission by any male person of any act of gross indecency with another male person, shall be guilty of a misdemeanour, and being convicted thereof shall be liable at the discretion of the court to be imprisoned for any term not exceeding two years, with or without hard labour.

Lesbian sexual practice has never been criminalised, which highlights the anxiety about men, rather than women, stepping outside their 'preordained' sexual roles and contaminating the law-makers themselves. It also reflects male disbelief in the existence of autonomous female desire and the possibility of non-phallic sexual acts. The association of homosexuality with the penis exacerbated the struggle for lesbian visibility – how to be validated when the law declares that you don't exist, yet you suffer discrimination and prejudice in every other sense? It has meant that lesbians have often fought alongside gay men in campaigns for homosexual rights which are constituted totally around men.

Homosexual women and homosexual men, femmes and faggots, queens, butches and dykes, we all fell under the rubric of gay: not simply an alliance of difference but an identification of sameness... And it founds the politics of my sexual identity squarely on a male paradigm. I was never in danger of being thrown into jail for practising sodomy, yet somehow the association with an outlaw sexuality defined my identity as dangerous.
Julia Creet, 'Outlook', No 11, Winter 1991

It was viewing Basil Dearden's 1961 film, *Victim*, again recently that re-inforced for me the horrific and lasting effects of the criminalisation of homosexuality – both in propagating lesbians' and gay men's fear of visibility and in legitimising homophobia. According to the film, over 80 per cent of blackmail cases at the time centred on the terrorisation of a 'queer victim'.

I spent the first twenty-five years of my life as a criminal. I remember dancing at the Slade with another man, which caused such shock. It was a real political intervention. That was enough of a commitment then. All the campaigning groups like CHE [Campaign for Homosexual Equality] were older and very straight-laced. Not until GLF [Gay Liberation Front] came along in 1971 was there a feeling of celebration. Derek Jarman

In the 1950s this courage to feel comfortable with arousing another woman became a political act. Joan Nestle, 'A Restricted Country'

It was not until 1954 that the Wolfenden Report was established to look into the legal position on homosexuality and it took a further three years to recommend that the law be changed. It was not until 1967 that sexual acts between consenting adult males in private were decriminalised, and even then the age of consent remained at twenty-one for gay male sex, whereas heterosexuals (and presumably lesbians) could fuck legally from the age of sixteen. The 1967 Act did not extend to the merchant marine or the armed forces. Nor did it cover Scotland or Northern Ireland, which clung to the standards of 1885 until 1980, when a Northern Irish gay man took the British government to the European Court of Human Rights and won his case. Over two decades after the decriminalisation of homosexuality, signs of 'sexual difference' are still greeted with denial and discrimination.

Glad to be gay

The early 70s saw a new, celebratory defiance by homosexuals, epitomised in Britain by the formation of the Gay Liberation Front and inspired to some extent by the determined mood of the Stonewall riots, which followed a police raid on one of New York's gay bars in 1969. 'Gay' was in, sorrow was out. And a new and powerful discourse which shunned the 'sick and sorry' attitude of some homosexuals began to develop, expressed through campaigns for equal rights, cultural recognition and sexual politics.

Gay liberation insisted... that what lesbians and gay men share is not some identical, *personal* essence of homosexual desire, but the social experience of discrimination and prejudice, which are mobilised by the workings of power – the law, the press, education, the Church, Social Services and so on – upon the terrain of sexuality *as a whole.*
Simon Watney

Just as queer politics perceives itself in opposition to the more assimilationist approaches of elements of lesbian and gay politics such as the Stonewall Group, GLF too saw itself as revolutionary compared to the homophile campaigns for civil rights of the 50s and 60s.

Borrowing from the rhetoric of the New Left, radical feminism, and black militant groups, young Gay Power activists saw their goal as the overthrow of an oppressive system of sex roles and family structure which had made heterosexuality compulsory. Elaine Showalter, 'Sexual Anarchy'

For many lesbians, feminism in the 70s became a more important political identity than gayness, and women began to split off from GLF to fight for the political acknowledgement of lesbians in the Women's Liberation Movement.

There were massive objections when lesbians threatened to come out publicly on the 1970 International Women's Day march in Boston, like we were giving feminism a bad name. Betty Friedan was interviewed and said, 'I will not be cowed by the Lavender Menace'. In one of our first collectives there was a Kathy Queer. The first gay publication, which came out twice, was called *Lavender Menace*. We put it together with a group of drag queens who called themselves queer too. Spike Pittsberg

Other lesbians, such as Joan Nestle, describe themselves as moving from the 'queer fifties', through the 'lesbian sixties' to the 'feminist seventies', where they experienced much of their lifestyles and identities being trashed by the new wave of feminism.

The word 'queer' is seen as a male word, or is so removed from the liberating energies of Lesbian-feminism that it makes me feel like a relic from another time... But... I need to remember what it was like to fight for sexual territory

in the time of McCarthy... to keep alive the memory that in the 1940s doctors measured the clitorises and nipples of Lesbians to prove our biological strangeness... My roots lie in the history of a people who were called freaks. Joan Nestle, 'A Restricted Country'

Dangerous days

The late 80s bred a distinct impatience with lesbian and gay integrationist strategies together with a frustration with the tyranny of political correctness imposed by local-authority lesbian and gay services. The widespread de-funding of the lesbian and gay voluntary sector in the post-GLC era meant reduced resources for lesbian and gay initiatives, and the resultant feeling of having been betrayed by both Labour and Tory parties helped to fuel the politics of assertion.

The AIDS crisis in Britain brought much latent homophobia to the surface, exacerbated by ill-advised safer sex campaigns and calls for the quarantine of people with AIDS. Lesbians were not considered a 'risk group' and many of us discovered more about safer sex practices from US pub-lications like Pat Califia's *Lesbian SM Safety Manual* than from the coy material produced by local Health Education Authorities.

In March 1987 ACT UP (AIDS Coalition to Unleash Power) was formed in New York, calling itself 'a diverse, nonpartisan group united in anger and committed to direct action to end the AIDS crisis'. The imaginative energy and fury which fuelled the AIDS movement in the US undoubtedly inspired some of the tactics used in Britain against the most insidious homophobic attack from the Tory government: Clause 28 of the Local Government Bill, which reads:

A local authority shall not:
(a) intentionally promote homosexuality or publish material with the intention of promoting homosexuality;
(b) promote the teaching in any maintained school of the acceptability of homosexuality as a pretended family relationship.

Despite huge and varied protests by lesbians, gay men and supportive heterosexuals, the Clause went into effect on 24 May 1988.

My actions were motivated wholly by the principle of supporting normality... Homosexuality is being promoted at the ratepayers' expense, and the traditional family as we know it is under attack. Tory MP David Wilshire, who proposed Clause 28, 'Guardian', 12 December 1987

Lesbians, inspired by tactics developed in the Greenham Common anti-nuclear protests, achieved maximum visibility by abseiling into the House of Lords and chaining themselves to newsreader Sue Lawley's desk, thereby interrupting the BBC's *Six O'Clock News*. The indignant anger behind the campaign against the Clause was not to die away.

Gay activists said this weekend that Clause 28 supporters may have scored an own goal. 'Putting Clause 28 through Parliament was one of the greatest promotions of homosexuality we have ever seen.'
'Sunday Times', 29 May 1991

The political strategies and unapologetic, aggressive, sex-positive attitude of ACT UP New York were adopted by ACT UP London, founded in January 1989. The new politics and tactics took the largely complacent medical establishment, as well as the lesbian and gay movement, by storm.

Yet the way AIDS was mythologised as a 'gay plague' continued. (Joke: What does 'gay' mean? – Got AIDS Yet?) The coy misinformation of government health campaigns did little to disseminate life-saving information; meanwhile, the continued association of AIDS with all gays served to legitimise physical, verbal and constitutional attacks on gay men and to a lesser extent lesbians, creating increased feelings of vulnerability. Remember Norwich Health Authority's refusal to allow lesbians to register to donate blood?

Clause 28 also legitimised homophobia. Numerous organisations lost their funding and lesbian and gay exhibitions and film screenings were banned by several regional authorities. In October 1989, for example, a group exhibition called 'Ecstatic Antibodies: Resisting the AIDS Mythology' was cancelled in Salford. The City Council officers invoked Section 28 to justify censoring homoerotic work which they declared pornographic and unsuitable for a 'family gallery'. Concern about promoting homosexuality in schools led two women teachers to be sacked from a Home Counties school for 'kissing in the school car park', after having received a warning against 'pursuing a personal relationship'. They were close friends but did not have a sexual relationship with each other. One of the women was heterosexual.

The time was ripe for a continued upsurge of lesbian and gay anger. In the wake of over a decade of the highly oppressive Thatcher regime, and in the midst of a mega-recession, there was a choice to buckle under, survive the mortgage movement, or explode. Queer activism is that explosion.

What is this thing called queer?

❝ *Queer means to fuck with gender. There are straight queers, bi-queers, tranny queers, lez queers, fag queers, SM queers, fisting queers in every single street in this apathetic country of ours.*❞
Anonymous leaflet: 'Queer Power Now', London 1991

❝ *Queer is a symptom, not a movement, a symptom of a desire for radical change.*❞ Keith Alcorn, 'Pink Paper', Issue 208

In April 1990 a group met in New York to discuss the frequent bashings of gays and lesbians in the East Village. Queer Nation was born with the slogan, 'Queers Bash Back' and stencils were drawn on the pavements: 'My beloved was queerbashed here. Queers fight back.' In classic postmodern fashion, Queer Nation borrowed styles and tactics from popular culture, black liberation struggles, hippies, AIDS activists, feminists and the peace movement to build its confrontational identity.

Queer Nationals are torn between affirming a new identity – 'I am queer' – and rejecting restrictive identities – 'I reject your categories'; between rejecting assimilation – 'I don't need your approval, just get out of my face' – and wanting to be recognised by mainstream society – 'we queers are gonna get in your face'. 'Outlook', No 11, Winter 1991

In London, OutRage was formed a few weeks later, with a similar 'in your face' agenda. **It was time.**
OutRage defines itself as:

A broad-based group of lesbians and gay men committed to radical non-violent direct action and civil disobedience to:
- *assert the dignity, pride and human rights of lesbians and gay men*
- *fight homophobia, discrimination and violence against lesbians and gay men*
- *affirm the rights of lesbians and gay men to sexual freedom, choice and self-determination.*

OutRage's first year produced a mass KISS-IN in Piccadilly Circus and a Queer Wedding in Trafalgar Square and provided plenty of sexy copy for a British press that had increasingly ignored or trivialised gay and lesbian politics.

Meanwhile, the legal system was introducing plenty of new challenges around which to rally disaffected queers. In December 1990, fifteen gay men were convicted on a series of charges for having **consensual** SM sex – a case that became known as Operation Spanner after the police code-name. In February 1992 their appeals were quashed. And in early 1991 the government introduced Clause 25 (now Section 27) of the Criminal Justice Act, which imposes stiffer sentences for certain sexual offences, including gay male procuring, solicitation and indecency, as well as child abuse, incest, rape, murder and sexual assault. The Clause was seen as the most serious move in over a century to increase the sentences for consenting homosexual behaviour and OutRage demonstrated outside Bow Street police station (chosen because it was where Oscar Wilde was charged almost 100 years ago), where activists 'turned themselves in' for crimes of importuning, indecency (kissing in the street) and procuring.

Legislation aimed at preventing lesbians from reproducing and lesbians and gay men from parenting also came to light. Paragraph 16 of the guidance notes to the 1989 Children Act contained an invidious little statement: '"Equal rights" and "gay rights" have no place in fostering', which was later amended, largely thanks to pressure from lesbian and gay campaigners. This followed closely on the Embryology Bill, which attempted to prevent lesbians using public A.I.D. services. The implication that only white, het, middle-class couples were fit parents had wide-reaching consequences for lesbian, gay, black and disabled parents, childcare workers, teachers and social services employees.

In March 1991, during the hysterical 'virgin births' furore about whether a woman who had not had penetrative sex with a man should be allowed artificial insemination, even the *Independent* newspaper supported the idea of dysfunctional lesbians:

How far is it reasonable to assume, on the basis of what we know of human psychology, that a woman who's been unable to establish a relationship with a man, will relate any better to a child?

For many woman, lesbian or not, it has often amounted to the same thing.

OutRage rallied against all three threats and over 10,000 marched to Hyde Park in protest. In covering the event, an allegedly liberal, quality newspaper wrote:

Not unexpectedly, the rally was addressed by a lesbian woman [sic] from Australia with a daughter produced by artificial insemination. The mother now faces deportation as an illegal immigrant. People do go to the ends of the earth in order to land up in the most extraordinary fixes.
'Observer', 10 March 1991

This sort of reporting reinforces the insidious moral code in Britain which suggests that:

- lesbians **choose** to fall in love with the wrong object choice in the wrong country (and that we certainly don't want to encourage any more of them pouring in from foreign places and getting away with it)
- the only healthy way to reproduce is by good old-fashioned 'planned' hetero-fucking and only then if both people are the same colour, race, class and age – note the frenzy when older women mate younger men
- people get arrested on peaceful demos because they choose to get in the policeman's way
- people die of AIDS because they have chosen to contract the disease

You just have to look at the way the press has been condoning the attacks on the transsexual hookers in the Bois de Boulogne. It is being talked about as if transsexuals from the Third World come to Paris out of sheer bloody-mindedness, and that somehow they are, of their nature, 'infected', and the punters are 'innocent victims' of these terrible people. Roz Kaveney

By mid-1991, OutRage had sprouted several affinity groups including the Whores of Babylon (Queers Fighting Religious Intolerance); SISSY (Schools Information Services on Sexuality); and PUSSY (Perverts Undermining State Scrutiny). Their often extravagant actions signalled the emergence of a highly ironic, camp, theatrical politics of direct action which bullied its way to the heart of the complacent media and put fun back into a wearied lesbian and gay movement. 'We've lobbied our tits off,' said Anna-Marie Smith, a founder member of PUSSY, 'and it didn't get us anywhere.'

Action vs assimilation

Tired of the gentlemanly approach, queer activists saw OutRage as distinctly anti-assimilationist compared to the parliamentary reform group, Stonewall, which had been established as a response to Clause 28 in 1989. The Stonewall agenda is described as:

To work for equality under the law and full social acceptance for lesbians and gay men. Our approach is an innovatory one for lesbian and gay rights – professional, strategic, tightly managed, able and willing to communicate with decision-makers in a constructive and informed way.
'Interim Report', The Stonewall Group, 1990

This much-criticised, self-elected group of twenty lesbians and gay men has never professed to be representative:

There really is no gay community. Most of us devise ways of keeping ourselves invisible. One feels one is on one's own.
Sir Ian McKellen, 'Independent on Sunday', 10 November 1991

But Stonewall has been perceived as the legitimate voice of the 'lesbian and gay community' by government ministers, though it did not succeed in using the fame or prestige of Sir Ian McKellen and many 'poofs with privilege' to resist Clause 28, or as yet to obtain an equal age of consent.

Assimilationist strategies have nonetheless worked in other European countries. In the Netherlands and Scandinavia, for example, the lesbian and gay community has achieved greater access to the state and has been able to push though an impressive range of legal and social rights. Legalised gay and lesbian weddings (as in Denmark) are far from my own reading of what constitutes equality, whether queer or not, but the acknowledgement of gay and lesbian sexuality in sex education signals the possibility of building a society with a greater tolerance of diversity. Will the fact that legal reforms are being achieved mean that there will not be the same need for queer politics in these countries?

OutRage activists are not interested in seeking acceptance within an unchanged social system, but are setting out to 'fuck up the mainstream' as visibly as possible. It can also be argued that the extremism of OutRage actually facilitates the gains of Stonewall, who are seen as 'rational' and 'civilised' in comparison.

In reality today, the main conflict is not simply between older 'gay' assimilationists... and 'queers' asserting their 'queerness'. Rather it is between those who think of the politics of sexuality as a matter of securing minority rights and those who are contesting the overall validity and authenticity of the epistemology of sexuality itself. Simon Watney

What's in a name?

Each time the word 'queer' is used it defines a strategy, an attitude, a reference to other identities and a new self-understanding. (And queer can be qualified as 'more queer', 'queerer' or 'queerest' as the naming develops into a more complex process of identification.) For many, the term marks a growing lack of faith in the institutions of the state, in political procedures, in the press, the education system, policing and the law. Both in culture and politics, queer articulates a radical questioning of social and cultural norms, notions of gender, reproductive sexuality and the family. We are beginning to realise how much of our history and ideologies operate on a homo-hetero opposition, constantly privileging the hetero perspective as normative, positing the homo perspective as bad and annihilating the spectrum of sexualities that exists.

I love queer. Queer is a homosexual of either sex. It's more convenient than saying 'gays' which has to be qualified, or 'lesbians and gay men'. It's an extremely useful polemic term because it is who we say we are, which is, 'Fuck You'. Spike Pittsberg

I use queer to describe my particular brand of lesbian feminism, which has not much to do with the radical feminism I was involved with in the early 80s.

I also use it externally to describe a political inclusivity – a new move towards a celebration of difference across sexualities, across genders, across sexual preference and across object choice. The two link. Linda Semple

I define myself as gay mostly. I will not use queer because it is not part of my vernacular – but I have nothing against its use. The same debates around naming occur in the 'black community'. Naming is powerful. Black people and gay people constantly renaming ourselves is a way to shift power from whites and hets respectively. Inge Blackman

What's in queer, for X, Y, Z, is mostly what people decide to make it. I like dyke and TS. Roz Kaveney

I don't use that term. I associate it with gay men and I'm dubious about reclaiming derogatory terms. The 'queer agenda', as you call it, isn't my struggle. I put my feminism before my lesbianism. Harriet Wistrich

I've got a badge that says QUEER BISEXUAL. Alison Thomas

I say 'I'm KHUSH', and that's from talking to Indian gay men and lesbians and finding that we want to find another word for ourselves that comes from our own culture. But I have used queer in the context of other queers. Pratibha Parmar

I'm more inclined to use the words 'black lesbian', because when I hear the word queer I think of white, gay men. Isling Mack-Nataf

Queer gives me politics for things I've always been interested in – like how I feel as a woman who's mistaken for a man, who's intrigued by men and gay male sexuality and as a lesbian and a feminist, connecting to my affinities with men's struggles around sexuality. Tori Smith

I do have problems with it, but I use queer in the sense that I'M FUCKED OFF, like 'faggots with attitude'. My anger has come from the work I've done around policing. I had no idea how outrageous it was. Paul Burston

I describe myself as a queer dyke. I never identified with the word lesbian because it seemed quite medical, it was the word I used to come out to my mother and it seemed to have negative connotations. Queer was one of the ways of identifying with a mixed movement and challenging both separatism and misogyny at the same time. Tessa Boffin

While there is resistance to the word queer, it is useful to remember that there were also battles over 'gay', which was not a term without contra-dictions. In the early 70s, gay too was characterised as radical and oppositional. By the 80s, lesbians felt the term had rendered them invisible and the addition of 'lesbians and' became a necessary part of naming. For some people who have come out since the beginning of the AIDS epidemic, there is a tendency to associate 'gay' with AIDS and to fail to identify with its happy subtext. However, criticism of the term is hardly new.

I never liked the word 'gay' (although I never said so), because it exuded a false optimism. It wasn't my word. I was in the party of miserabilists.
Derek Jarman

While some older gay liberationists claim that gay is the only way to be, their earnest defence of the term fails to acknowledge either the evolution of self-naming, or the experiences of a younger generation. One of the most vehement members of the anti-queer lobby is Chris White, whose 'Inrage' mounts a one-man picket, complete with a placard claiming 'Homosexuals Are Not Queer', outside the London Lesbian and Gay Centre to discourage people from attending OutRage meetings.

I shall continue to fight for as long as OutRage and their ilk believe it is part of their role to oppress us, split us and do our enemies' work for us.
Chris White, 'Capital Gay', 24 January 1991

The debate has certainly produced lively political exchanges in the letters' pages of the gay press. Yet although for some of the older generation, the term 'queer' painfully the recalls the homophobic abuse of a former era, for others it is merely a return to a word they used in a positive, self-parodying sense many years ago.

Back in the 60s when I was trying to figure out whether I was 'gay' or transsexual or what, the people I got to know in the TS/drag queen network in the north would use 'queer' in a 'what of it?' way. They'd sometimes use it in a self-deprecating manner and the two uses would shade into each other. 'Gay' was useful, but it changed nothing. The average homophobe uses it as derogatively as 'poofter' or 'homo'. It's just another word, it doesn't have intrinsic power for good. Roz Kaveney

Lesbians fight back

Queer politics is renowned for its sex-positive reclamation of words that have been used negatively against women and lesbians and gays, as well as for its outlandish acronyms. The OutRage affinity group, PUSSY (Perverts Undermining State Scrutiny) is a mixed gay and lesbian group set up to fight censorship, sexism and 'promote queer sex'. PUSSY's aim is to work actively to gain acknowledgement of lesbian sexual practices, both within and beyond the lesbian and gay community, rather than simply to campaign against prohibitive measures.

However, many of PUSSY's campaigns to date have been reactions to censorship from within the community – as in its organisation of protests when London gay and feminist bookshops Gay's the Word, Silver Moon and Sisterwrite refused to carry Della Grace's book *Love Bites* (although West & Wilde, the gay and lesbian bookshop in Edinburgh, and major bookshop chains stocked the title). PUSSY also worked to support the distribution of *Quim* (Britain's first lesbian sex mag), which encountered similar restrictions.

Other campaigns include defending the Terrence Higgins Trust's safer sex material and drawing attention to the Jenny White case. In 1991, White, a fifty-seven-year-old member of the London Older Lesbian Network, had ordered several porn tapes made by lesbians (Blush Productions and Fatale Videos) and sold through a lesbian sex shop in San Francisco. The tapes were seized by Customs and Excise and declared obscene, under the nineteenth-century law that prohibits the importation of 'obscene material'. With the support of FAC (Feminists Against Censorship) and PUSSY, White took the case to court, on point of principle, knowing that she would lose, but keen to highlight the inequality in the law. In court she explained that the videos were for private use and the depictions of safer sex and sexuality were less violent and 'obscene' than much of what is available through heterosexual outlets. The judge proceeded to view the most 'depraved, lewd and filthy' extracts and in a bizarre venture in voyeurism, lesbians in the gallery watched men watching lesbians. White's defence argued that it was absurd that these materials could be imported through the EC, but not from the US. It also seemed strange that this material was being banned, since many women had viewed at least two of the videos in screenings at the Rio cinema and National Film Theatre. Although the tapes were ordered to be destroyed, White did not have to pay costs and felt that this was a minor victory and could be claimed as a queer intervention into the anomalies of the law.

Your sexuality is yours. It's not the state's, the Customs Officer's, or your husband's. It's yours and its exploration with another person is the only way to claim your birthright. Jenny White

In November of the same year a legal precedent was established concerning lesbian sexual practices which could be seen as a measure of the virulent hostility the threat of queer sex invokes. Jennifer Saunders, an eighteen-year-old, was sentenced to six years' imprisonment for dressing as a man and seducing two seventeen-year-old women. The age of consent laws could not be used against her – again revealing the anomaly whereby lesbians remain invisible – and so she was charged with indecent assault. In court, the two women said they would not have consented to sex if they had been aware of Saunders' true gender; in her defence, Saunders insisted that she had dressed as a boy at the women's request, to conceal the fact that they were having a lesbian relationship. Passing sentence in Doncaster, Judge Crabtree summed up:

I suppose that both girls would rather have been raped by some young man ... I assume you must have some sort of bisexual feelings and I suspect that you have contested the case in the hope of getting some ghastly fame from it. I feel you may be a menace to young girls.

Saunders allegedly had sex with one of the women several times a week, using a strap-on dildo, in the course of a five-month affair. A new OutRage affinity group, LABIA (Lesbians Answer Back in Anger) took up the case and picketed the office of the Lord Chancellor to demand the dismissal of Judge Crabtree from the bench. In a letter to LABIA from prison, Saunders reiterated that the affairs were entirely consensual:

She told her family I was a man to make herself clear, if you know what I mean... I couldn't believe it when I was arrested. I went along with all the stupid things she was saying as I loved her more than anything in the world. I couldn't hurt her. So I promised to say nothing.

Without LABIA, the press would have ignored the fact that the case had anything to do with lesbians. And indeed there was a distinct failure of other lesbian feminist groups to rally to Saunders' defence – was this due to moral disapproval of the dildo or of the ultra-butch (ie perceived as het male) persona Saunders chose? In the same month as the case came to trial, there was a huge International Women's Day to End Violence Against Women march which focused on legal injustices to women. It highlighted the cases of Sara Thornton, Kiranjit Ahwalia and Amelia Rossiter, all of whom were given life sentences for killing their husbands. There was no mention of the Saunders' case in the publicity.

On the press front, the *Sun* not unexpectedly ran a headline: '6 Years for blonde who posed as boy to bed girls' (21 September 1991), while the *Guardian* ran a coy little piece on cross-dressing entitled 'Girls will be boys', in which Julie Wheelwright, author of *Amazons and Military Maids: Women Who Dressed as Men in Pursuit of Life, Liberty and Happiness*, opined that cross-dressing was a 'forgotten historical phenomenon', and concluded:

In the end, cross-dressing proves to be an unsatisfying alternative since it forces women to caricature male virility and fear their feminine self.
'Guardian', 24 September 1991

With moralising reactionary analysis like that, all butch women should forget it. The article omitted the 'L word' and made no attempt to discuss why teenagers had been forced to use such subterfuge in England in the late twentieth century: **homophobia**. Saunders' six-year sentence was longer than most rape sentences and it was clear that she was being punished for being a woman who dared to step out of line. At the time of writing Saunders is in Styal prison, awaiting appeal.

To out or not to out...

One of the most widely discussed queer strategies for the promotion of lesbian and gay visibility has been outing, which brought queer politics into the headlines and strongly divided opinion and support among lesbians and gay men. The FROCS (Faggots Rooting Out Closeted Sexuality) outing campaign of August 1991, which promised to out several MPs, gained more column inches for lesbian and gay politics in one week than in the whole of the previous year. The campaign was allegedly an elaborate hoax designed to highlight the hypocrisy of the tabloid press, who had been content to expose publicly whomsoever they could, yet now began to bleat about notions of 'privacy'.

For lesbians and gays, outing represented the nub of the queer debate. For many, like Derek Jarman, who argued that 'outing is a sign that the gay [sic] movement has come of age', it was a positive affirmation of the right to be open about sexuality by a new generation of lesbian and gay men who, content with their 'sexual orientation', were refusing to toe the line submissively, or accept discrimination and harassment. For others, the campaign raised moral, ethical and political questions. Could someone who'd been reluctantly dragged out of their closet represent a positive role model? Wasn't declaring Jason Donovan or Jodie Foster 'absolutely queer' fetishising the glamour of those in public positions and their power to influence opinion? The notion of 'claiming our own' makes the assumption that all queers are progressive, have an essential awareness of oppression and therefore sympathise with the queer cause; like 'gay lifestyle', it reinforces a spurious idea of lesbian and gay homogeneity. And while many yearn to reveal politicians' hypocrisy, whipping up homophobia to discredit them can only be destructive and ultimately counter-productive. Using outing as punishment raises the question of who was choosing to out whom?

The campaign denied the levels of coming out we all have to consider – the closet door often revolves – and ignored the different contexts for women and black people, for whom being lesbian or gay intersects with the oppressions of sexism and racism. Are you more queer the more outspoken you can risk being? The more visible? The more vulnerable?

Many of the younger Asian men and women in their early twenties I speak to are saying 'we're not interested in coming out that way, because if we do we won't have anywhere to live, we'll be chucked out from home'. It's not about their lack of confidence about their sexuality, it's about what choices are available. That's something that's always been seen by white lesbians and gay men as 'behind'. It creates a certain kind of hierarchy from a white perspective and a white agenda.
Pratibha Parmar

The separatism of the outing campaign made no room for heterosexual or bisexual anti-homophobes and in many ways went against queer ethics in its reinforcement of the normative categories of the homo-hetero divide. We constantly negotiate the territory in which it is safe and appropriate to come out, so it follows that there are times when queers may choose to call themselves heterosexual, bisexual, lesbian or gay, or none of the above. If queer develops into an anti-straight polemic, it will have betrayed its potential for radical pluralism. Nor can you simply substitute 'queer' for 'gay' and masquerade reactionary politics under a radical new guise.

The 'bad' girls

The attraction of queer for some lesbians is flavoured by a rebellion against a prescriptive feminism that had led them to feel disenfranchised by the lesbian feminist movement. There was a feeling that the importance of identifying politically as a lesbian had obscured lesbianism as a sexual identity. 'Acceptable' ideas of lesbian sexuality and desire were constructed around notions of sameness and a desexed androgyny, and anyone who disagreed with the 'right on' line, regardless of her sexual practice, would be dismissed at best as an SM dyke and at worst as a fascist. While the ground gained by identity politics in promoting equal representation and access to resources were important achievements of feminism, the rigid hierarchies of oppression rhetoric that privileged certain oppressions above others were considered divisive and futile.

As a black lesbian, feminism let me down a lot, especially when debates stuck to gender and didn't include race or 'other' sexual practices. I want a context to look at more diversity. Isling Mack-Nataf

Feminism as it has evolved can no longer accept difference and can only accept an orthodoxy that enforces 'if you don't fit that orthodoxy, you're not only wrong, you're dangerous'. Linda Semple

The feminist movement was divided into the good, the bad and the ugly. The bad were women who fucked around but had serial monogamy and a sense of sex that had to do with love. The ugly were the women who were seen as male and had a sense of sex that had to do with consent. Queer was a way of retrieving that, of risking, of knowing there's no such thing as safe sex. There's safer sex. Sue Golding

AIDS activism is far more effective than feminism ever was because it allows a broad diversity of opinion, while in feminism there was a tendency to block a range of analysis. Sarah Schulman

Discussions around HIV and safer sex soon highlighted the lack of information available on lesbian sexual practice. *The Joy of Lesbian Sex* was no longer in print and few booksellers would risk stocking the sex mag *On Our Backs*. The success of anti-porn campaigns had ensured that access to books like *Coming To Power* (SAMOIS) or *Sapphistry* (Pat Califia) was severely limited. (One bookseller told how she would find such volumes turned spine inwards or hidden behind more politically correct (PC) literature.) Perhaps there was something to be learned from a new generation of gay men who were rejecting the apologetic reactions and confused recommendations of abstention that had characterised the beginning of the AIDS epidemic and asserting a new confidence. If they had to fuck safely, they certainly weren't going to apologise for their desire.

Dykes had to take the models of gay male sexual practice, apply them to

lesbian sexual practice and say, 'what if?' There was an intellectual
and theoretical need to ally with gay men around the politics of
representation and sexuality which had been hijacked by radical
lesbian feminists. Linda Semple

*For gay men the situation is 'we'll tolerate you being homos as long as you
aren't sexual'. I'm going to be 'homo' and 'sexual'.* Paul Burston

For other lesbians, queer has little to do with gay men; its roots are firmly
embedded in the dyke camp, with its history of cross-dressing, role-playing,
gender-fucking and subversion of patriarchy. The writings of women like Joan
Nestle, Carole Vance, Gayle Rubin and Ann Snitow are considered some of
the queerer elements to emerge from feminism.

Queer is a function of the debates around sexuality which were started
by lesbians. We pushed back the borders and talked about SM, fantasies,
taboos, butch-femme, violence in relationships, non-monogamy,
penetration, ass-fucking etc. Many of us were doing it before HIV forced
us to. Spike Pittsberg

*We Lesbians from the fifties made a mistake in the early seventies: we allowed
our lives to be trivialised and reinterpreted by feminists who did not share our
culture. The slogan 'Lesbianism is the practice and feminism is the theory' was
a good rallying cry, but it cheated our history... For many years now, I have
been trying to figure out how to explain the special nature of butch-femme
relationships to Lesbian-feminists who consider butch-femme a reproduction
of heterosexual models.* Joan Nestle, 'A Restricted Country'

*One thing I hope as a historian is that the fact that feminists pioneered a lot
of queer ideas doesn't get lost, so it becomes seen as something that only
grew out of ACT UP or men's ideas.* Tori Smith

Queer seems as chameleon as camp, which is also a useful vehicle for self-
understanding and reading the signs of the moment, also labelled as self-
oppressive. At times, the two interlink; certainly both can be viewed as
subjective reinterpretations of the times, whether in art, politics or as a means
of self-understanding.

    For me, the taking back of negative words has been a survival strategy.
I came out in the early 80s, when all the words available to me to articulate
my desire were constructed negatively: lesbian, lessie, dyke ('gay' was never
an option for self-naming as it was seen as definitively male in my radical
feminist milieu), cunt, pussy, fuck... Or the words were non-existent: I didn't
know I possessed a clitoris until I was eighteen. I was supposed to play with
'my bits', stroke someone else's and separate from all emotional and physical
contact with men. I did. It has been a long haul back to reclaiming the right
to call my cunt, my cunt, to celebrating the pleasure in objectifying another
body, to fucking women and to admitting that I also love men and need
their support. That is what queer is.

Whose agenda is it?

❝ *By building an identity exclusively around one sexuality and developing a political agenda that either excludes or subordinates other forms of oppression, the lesbian and gay movement has narrowly defined its subject.***❞**
Charles Fernandez, 'Outlook', Spring 1991

Queer is welcomed as breaking up lesbian and gay orthodoxies and making possible new alliances across gender and other disparate identities; it is claimed by some as neutral in terms of race and gender. But is the umbrella as all-embracing as queer claims? Are we in danger of denying our heterogeneity in favour of a false 'queer nationalism'?

I think that too much emphasis on 'queer nation' is itself a new kind of separatism and can lead in the direction of an equally narrow politics in which queers become the new 'most of all oppressed' group. I'm opposed to separatism of any kind, whether it's lesbian, black, Muslim or anything else. Elizabeth Wilson

One of the challenges that each new generation of lesbians and gay men faces is how to build on the gains and experience of previous movements. Queer rhetoric often gives the impression that direct action politics was invented in 1987, that the Black and Women's Liberation Movements haven't happened, that the campaigns for or against nuclear weapons, abortion, reproductive rights and violence against women have not occurred and have had no influence on the way queer activism manifests itself. But despite the inevitable frustration experienced by more seasoned campaigners, there is also a celebration of the fact that a new generation of gay and lesbian activists is resurrecting old debates in new contexts and formulating new debates in old contexts they believe to be new.

It's infuriating to re-invent the wheel, to see people make the same mistakes we made fifteen years ago. We don't have a proper way of passing on skills. Lisa Power

Working with men

Queer has enabled many of the discussions that were happening in single-sex spaces to be continued in mixed public contexts for the first time in many years. (This had, of course, been happening in private all along, as dykes and faggots swopped cruising disasters with cottaging tales and was a feature of groups of the 70s which sound remarkably familiar – for example, DAFT: Dykes And Faggots Together.) But many lesbians who worked with men in the years before the AIDS crisis were branded as 'bad' lesbians by their peers.

I had worked with gay men on 'Ecstatic Antibodies' and there was a lot of unease about it. People didn't say anything to my face, but I heard of comments that I was getting where I was because I was arse-licking men. Tessa Boffin

Of course, ridding men of misogyny and creating a mutual confidence whereby lesbians no longer need to separate from men to define their own agendas is a difficult process. Are gay men in mixed queer settings willing to listen and be challenged?

Gay men can learn from dykes what it's like to be a woman, the reality, not the fantasy. They can listen and learn that being a man means they are automatically given many privileges which are not open to women. They should learn how lesbophobic they are. It's not just as simple as being misogynistic, which a lot of them are, but their active fear, dislike and loathing of LESBIANS. Inge Blackman

There's a brand of boy around at the moment who reckon that just because you're a pro-sex dyke, maybe don a bit of leather... you have forgotten your feminism and they can get away with sexist put downs, anti-women jokes and all the rest. It's as if they think there are two kinds of dykes the 'old kind' who got on their nerves with their 'excuse me that's the third time you've interrupted me' and some new kind which they reckon is me. I've been... with gay men who assumed, until set straight, that they could get snide about the 'feminist kind of lesbian' and I'd laugh along. 'Quim', Winter 1991

Other women members of OutRage have complained about the 'faggot cringe' response, whereby gay men seem to assume that anything a dyke says should be accepted without criticism. Overall, however, it seems that many of the white gay men drawn to OutRage because of the increased levels of queer-bashing have only recently become aware of the street violence and harassment that women and black men and women have always suffered. A 'Condom Patrol' organised to give out safer sex materials on Hampstead Heath pointed up some of the differences in perspective. When lesbians bemoaned the lack of cottaging for lesbians, men suggested they went to the Heath too.

I said to them, 'What about safety?' and they said, 'oh yeah'. It was pretty remarkable to be in a park after midnight and not feel scared for the first time in my life. Tori Smith

For many gay men who felt constructed as the enemy or simply irrelevant to previous feminist discourses, working with dykes on queer issues has been a valuable process. Lesbians who've been involved with feminism are more familiar with making links between theories of representation and practice, and are offering a broad experience of political organising to queer campaigns.

I've gained a broader overview of political structures and the ways that our sexuality is oppressed. I can recognise now that it isn't simply to do with gay male issues, like getting arrested for wanking in a public toilet. Paul Burston

One of the things that could emerge from queer is gay men seeing their own practices, styles and culture taken over by dykes and then reflected back with inflections and criticisms. The danger being that reciprocity won't operate in quite this way, and at worst, gay men will glory in the fact that at last 'lesbians have seen the light, owned up to their mistakes and come back to what are considered correct queer political and cultural practices'. Philip Derbyshire

Despite the initial idea of queer politics as a movement in which men and women would work together and learn from each other, groups such as DAM (Dyke Action Machine) in New York and the LABIA groups in San Francisco and London have been set up to focus on women's issues. Isn't setting up a lesbian caucus within OutRage admitting that the agenda is controlled by men's concerns? There seemed a danger in 1991 that campaigns about sex (Clause 25) were perceived as men's and campaigns about parenting (Paragraph 16) as women's. And on a practical level, the group's failure to organise a crèche attracted widespread, justified criticism. But is it also the case that lesbians have yet to initiate a queer agenda that is proactive rather than a reaction to feelings of exclusion?

It's how to be involved in a movement that makes you invisible and ignores you. We want to be in the queer movement, but it's still on the level of having to ask men to include us. Della Grace

Oppression infantalises people. There's been a tradition in the past few years of women telling other women not to do things, like work with men, but people are not starting activist groups based on women's issues. They're only starting them in response to men not fulfilling their needs and that's because people haven't figured out what a lesbian agenda is. Last year I called a meeting for lesbians to start a direct action group and I got 150 women. Half of them were ready to go to work and the other half had come to stop the first half from doing it. It was that fear of action (as opposed to being reactive) and the destructive critical tradition. Sarah Schulman

I get annoyed when OutRage says 'this is a lesbian action' because queer actions should cross both sexes. The lesbian action was the most boring one they had. Tessa Boffin

But whatever its short-term (or longer-term) failures, queer does signal that discussions between lesbians and gay men – until recently marked by their absence, hostility or accusatory approach – are now beginning to be framed by mutual curiosity and responsibility. There is still a lot we don't know or understand about our distinct sexual, political and cultural histories. Queer presents the possibility and challenge to find out.

Yet another whitewash?

While for some white lesbians it feels like a radical renaissance to work with men, black lesbians did not buy into the separatist agenda in quite the same way in the first place, often choosing to align with black men, both straight and gay, to counter the racism they encountered in the feminist and gay movements. Now black lesbians are organising largely around cultural groups like Shakti, the South Asian lesbian and gay network, rather than with queer-identified groups. While many feel sympathetic towards the aims of OutRage, some of its actions – for example the 'Turn-In' outside Bow Street police station – are seen as inappropriate. Just as the feminist 'Reclaim the Night' marches of the 80s demanded that all men get off the streets, thus alienating black women who were fighting for the right of black people to walk the streets day and night without harassment, so an action which involves offering yourself up for arrest to a police force renowned for its violent racism is not the best way to achieve broad-based support.

Queer Nation politics are crudely similar to the Malcolm X, Black Panther type of black politics. It's exciting and sexy. On the surface! But in any heterogeneous group there is always a group of people who rise to the top, who hijack the agenda. In the women's movement, it's white middle-class women (still), in the black movement, black heterosexual men (still), so with OutRage, white gay men. I don't care to join groups in which I have to fight to be heard. Inge Blackman

The coalitional work still needs to happen and trust needs to be built before the diversity of the lesbian and gay community can come together and work under the umbrella term of queer. A lot of that groundwork has not been done and is not seen as important enough in the rush to claim a word that is all-embracing. Pratibha Parmar

It is significant that the American phrase 'Queer Nation' has not been taken up to the same extent in Britain, perhaps because the term 'Nation' for African Americans has more direct links with past liberation struggles. For some it described the idea of seceding a couple of states to create a homogeneous paradise; for others it was more of a Pan-African association. In urban ghettos there were the beginnings of the creation of a Black Nation to meet economic and social needs. It was a term concerned with affirming an abused culture and identity.

In Britain, by contrast, the word 'nation' has associations with the National Front and British National Party and the fascist nationalist agenda.

When I was growing up in the States, the idea of Black Nationalism was very important for disenfranchised black people. It was an effort to decondition self-hate and get white capitalist ideology out of our heads. When people asked you the time, you'd reply, 'It's "Nation Time"' to remind ourselves that, if we all agreed, we could bring about a Black Nation now. Isling Mack-Nataf

What time was it? Certainly not 'Nation Time' not for this young, gifted, Black – and queer! – student. No nation, however revolutionary had dared claim me. Marlon Riggs, 'Outlook', Spring 1991

I find the word 'Nation' problematic because I'm against many nationalisms and essentialisms. There's been an upsurge in nationalism in the black and lesbian and gay communities in the UK because these communities have been under attack. Isaac Julien

Part of what black people, Jewish people and other non-whites struggled for in the 60s and 70s was the right to retain their cultural distinctness. 'Gay' or 'lesbian' may not be the primary basis of their identity, and to take on the label 'queer' is seen as a 'whitewashing' of their existence.

I don't want to get homogenised and deny my difference, which I assert as a very conscious choice. My Jewish lesbian group is connected to the synagogue, identity and culture, but I wouldn't say that as lesbians we've got much in common. Ruth Novazcek

The problem is that if one has an identification that is so fixed that it excludes change and negotiation with other identities, then I still need to come together with other black lesbians and create a culture. Isling Mack-Nataf

Some black lesbians foresee similar problems with queer as they experienced with white Western feminism, which often tried to prescribe feminist practices for women in developing countries, taking no account of the historical, social or cultural context. There is also a fear that white queer groups will be privileged as more visible and 'radical', thus undermining and rendering invisible equally queer black campaigns. An example of such a campaign, though it didn't use the word 'queer', was the Black Lesbians and Gays Against Media Homophobia's action against *The Voice* newspaper's homophobic reporting, which had culminated in an attack on black gay footballer, Justin Fashanu, who had come out to the *Sun* in the previous week. Using a front-page headline quote from John Fashanu, 'My gay brother is an outcast', *The Voice* claimed:

Homosexuals are the greatest 'queerbashers'... they feel guilty... should go back into the closet... because we heteros are sick and tired of tortured queens. 'The Voice', 30 October 1990

The Black Lesbians and Gays Against Media Homophobia co-ordinated a nine-month boycott of the paper (Britain's largest black-owned business) and finally they and Fashanu were granted space to respond. The full-page right of reply came with superb anti-homophobic remarks from both Huey P. Newton, Commander of the Black Panther Party, and Angela Davis. The article drew parallels between racism and homophobia:

Black people are so often stereotyped, particularly by the media, as criminals or loveless lechers that the impression has stuck in the minds of many people. Similar myths are spread about lesbians and gays... Racist 'Christians' use the Bible to incorrectly call our ancestors 'primitive, godless savages'... In the same way homophobic Christians use the Bible... If our sense of community as Black lesbians and gays is under threat – as indeed it is – then the whole community is threatened. 'The Voice', 29 October 1991

Definitely one of the queerest things to hit the British press that year.

I felt totally liberated by that intervention. The interventions by black lesbians and gays are different because there are different communities of interest. Now *The Voice* has to watch it! Isaac Julien

Queer credentials

One of the founding aims of Queer Nation was to incorporate bisexuals into the lesbian and gay movement. (It now seems totally bizarre that until recently bisexuals were not allowed to join the London Lesbian and Gay Centre.) Do bisexuals feel part of a new Queer Nation?

OutRage meets in the Lesbian and Gay Centre, but you can be straight and queer. They're not addressing that issue. Queer here is a long way behind the States in terms of accepting bisexuals. The subgroups in Queer Nation there are less divisive. LABIA there stands for 'Lesbians and Bisexuals In Action', while here LABIA represents 'Lesbians Answer Back In Anger'. Alison Thomas

Now, as opposed to the mid-80s, I feel able to relax about my sexuality for the first time – partly because of the SM row, and more openness around bisexuality, and partly because people are talking more about sexual practice. But we have to wait and see how inclusive queer is. Bisexuals seem less apologetic, but there are two kinds of bi-activists – those who are out bi's and lesbians and gays who have a guilty secret. Several transsexuals I know don't want anything to do with lesbian and gay politics because they had their fingers burnt. There's nothing like being told to go home and commit suicide to put you off political activism for life. Roz Kaveney

At the march against Clause 28, 90 per cent of the people there were gay men. I got very upset when a friend said, 'You see Tilda, it really is a gay issue'. Separatism is a dangerous thing to get into in England because the English are so good at it. Tilda Swinton, 'Spare Rib', June 1988

I don't think I could claim queer. If somebody wanted to call me queer I'd be quite happy about it, but I still feel it's about who you sleep with. I often talk about being a mother in my writing, but consciously never say whether I'm straight or gay. While I want to embrace queer politics, some of the very basic demands of the Women's Liberation Movement have to be met – like childcare – but that's not very queer is it? Not very exciting? Suzanne Moore

Critics of OutRage argue that the movement is in danger of a typically postmodern slippage from ethics to aesthetics, with activists claiming entry not on the grounds of their political awareness, but on superficial self-presentation. Could this develop into a fashion-led prescriptiveness, whereby people decide who is queer by their haircut or choice of jacket (black leather being the only iconographic signifier of note), with the biggest topic on the agenda being which is the hippest club to cruise at later?

Some older dykes feel inspired by the direct action politics, but intimidated by the trendy style of baby activists; for others, it is precisely that energy and freshness that is appealing. Some younger lesbians and gay men feel they can make more comfortable alliances with each other than with older gay men, who seem complacent, or older lesbians, who have been through the separatist and SM wars and have now nested in monogamous mortgaged assimilation, with promise of a child to come.

Queer is in danger of going the same way as Punk – a movement with the potential to incite radical social change, squatted by careerists and fashion-victims and reduced to a few slogans.
Paul Burston, 'Kennedy's Gay Guide', December 1991

I worry about the word queer. I still have this image of the gay clone in a black leather jacket and shaved 'blonde' head and I worry that it will perpetuate that aesthetic. Ruth Novazcek

It's strange to see gay skinheads and I have to negotiate that. Although I have difficulty (as it not only points to a fascist aesthetic, it also wants to undermine it) I don't want to avoid those difficulties. Isling Mack-Nataf

An Asian guy told me that one of the things he finds exciting about queer politics is that he's always liked dressing up in saris and feels that, in the past, not only did he have people from his own culture saying,

'that's effeminate nonsense', but he had white feminists saying, 'you can't do this, it's really offensive'. Now he can dress up, go to the Asia club and dance. Linda Semple

There is still little mention of how disabled queers fit into the queer agenda, although a small caucus called LINK exists at OutRage to discuss these issues. It is probably because many disabled lesbians and gays are still trying to fight for a way into both the homophobic disability movement (of course people with disabilities are sexual, we're normal, have normal het desires like you and want normal families too...) and the largely inaccessible venues in which much of the lesbian and gay community congregates. Once again disability could provide a site for revolutionising the way normative notions of physical and sexual types are reinforced.

The map of the new queer nation would have a male face and mine and those of many of my sisters of colour would be simply background material. We would be the demographic cosmetics, as it were, to assuage and complement the deeply embedded prejudices and unself-conscious omissions of so many angry young men. Maria Maggenti, 'Outlook', Winter 1991

So how does OutRage work? The energy is inspirational, the enthusiasm refreshing and the language and procedures unique – including the vibe monitors, appointed to keep an eye on the levels of aggression and hostility and declare when it's time to cool off... However at several meetings I attended it appeared that it wasn't only the law for whom lesbians are invisible. The only issue of lesbian equality on the agenda was lesbian custody, and there seemed a common assumption that the women present would have a thought-through agenda, with more experience and interest than the men. At another meeting A.I.D. was classed as a lesbian issue – where, pray, does the sperm come from? 'Lesbian issues' seemed to be tagged on to the end of agendas and invariably postponed until the following week, due to lack of time. And the money for T-shirts had been used up before the dyke T-shirts could be printed.

Was it déjà vu? While queer raises the possibility of dealing with complex subjectivities and differences in terms of gender, race and class, it also risks not trying hard enough to resist the reductive prescriptiveness some of us suffered in feminism and the uncritical essentialism that privileges the queerness of gay white men. While it offers lesbians an escape from unilateral lesbian orthodoxy into a more pluralistic and flexible politics, there is a danger of losing sight of the progressive aspects of feminism, which gave many of us the courage to speak.

Transgression or chickenshit?

❛ *OutRage is all about challenging the concept that your sexuality is defined by the gender of the person you sleep with. It's not.* ❜ Chris Woods, 'Independent on Sunday', 10 November 1991

❛ *Question: "When does a lesbian boy become a man?" Answer : "She doesn't."* ❜ Della Grace

Is straight SM automatically queer, while a monogamous 'vanilla' lesbian couple living in suburbia isn't? How many SM dykes on the scene consider themselves queer and are involved in street actions? Just as the lesbian sex wars created false polarities between the anti-censorship, sex-positive gang and the anti-sex, pro-censorship lobby, so there is a danger that queer, with an agenda seen as promoting sexual transgression, will occupy one camp, while 'lesbian and gay' takes up the other, with no space to move between.

I don't like this outlawism around sexuality. It's a whole new sexual policing. What's transgressive to one person is offensive to another and chickenshit to another. Spike Pittsberg

The gender-polarised feminism of the 60s and 70s blocked any attempts to understand how lesbian and gay male desires and identities might be mapped against each other. Lesbian sex was posited as loving and mono-gamous, in false opposition to gay male sex, which was deemed abusive, exploitative and promiscuous. The split was compounded by a moralistic feminist separatism that declared that the further women got from the penis, the better lesbians they became. Many gay men felt that their sexual practices and ethics were reviled and policed, thereby blocking almost all discussion about shared oppression. The situation for black lesbians and gay men, as outlined in the previous chapter, was often different as the fight against racism was given priority.

At the same time, lesbian feminism rejected modes of behaviour and appearance that were encoded as 'feminine', idealising instead an androgyny (based on a masculine aesthetic) that was somehow promoted as both 'natural' and progressive. Butch and femme were outlawed as a replay of heterosexist power imbalances. The silencing of anything but 'right on' forms of sexual expression led to a failure to negotiate issues of desire and power, as lesbian feminists propagated the belief that women did not objectify each other sexually and that lust was a gentle wild orchid. The anxiety about what constituted correct 'feminist' sexual desire resulted, in extreme cases, in a ludicrous sexual code that forbade even finger penetration.

Pornography and the SM wars

One of the key sites of the battles between feminists was, and continues to be, pornography. To watch, never mind admit to enjoying porn, was deemed equal to treacherous collusion with the most sinister component of hetero-patriarchy. Anti-porn campaigners often conflated sexually explicit images with violence against women, so that instead of analysing the social construction of male sexual violence, campaigns focused on the battle for censorship, even though the links between male violence and pornography are far from proven. Perhaps because porn is visible and explicit, it became an easy target on which to focus the fight against sexism and racism.

However, the feminist debate around pornography did lead to several important, if unintentional gains:

- in a society where the language available to women to articulate their sexuality is severely limited, the debates gave them the opportunity to develop means of talking explicitly and publicly about sexual practice
- a demand for explicit information on and cultural representation of lesbian sexual practices, by and for lesbians, was created
- the notion of the pure lesbian who only indulges in equal, nurturing, prepubescent sex, was challenged
- alliances between pro-sex anti-censorship lesbians and like-minded gay men were fostered, so opening up the possibility of new models for the expansion of lesbian erotic possibilities
- the radical, anti-censorship, feminist lobby FAC (Feminists Against Censorship) was formed

The challenge for queer politics is to continue to build on these gains.

In 1984, anti-pornographers Andrea Dworkin and Catherine McKinnon introduced the Minneapolis Ordinance, which allowed women to take civil action against anyone involved in the production, sale or distribution of pornography on the grounds that the prosecutor had been harmed by the image of women's sexuality portrayed. The definition of pornography was dangerously broad, and the alliance of the campaign with the American right was a worrying indicator of what might follow. FACT (Feminist Anti-Censorship Task Force) was set up in the US and FAC (Feminists Against Censorship) was founded in London in 1989. FAC's first leaflet argued: 'We need a feminism willing to tackle issues of class and race and to deal with the variety of oppressions in the world, not to reduce all oppressions to pornography.'

For some lesbian feminists, the threat of increased censorship at a time of new openness in the discussion of sexual practice and a newly created demand for and production of sexually explicit material was **bad news**. The nub of the censorship debate for dykes came in 1985, when the London Lesbian and Gay Centre (now the site of a blooming mixed SM club... due to queer, or simply the weariness of the radfem lobby?) declared that SM groups and anyone wearing 'SM clothes' would be banned. (Although access was finally won, even as recently as March 1991, a gay man wearing half a handcuff on his leather jacket was denied entry. The fact that he lost the other half to the Metropolitan Police while participating in an AIDS demo was considered irrelevant.)

It is important to highlight the SM sex battle as it signifies why so many dykes developed a dissatisfaction and disaffection for 'lesbian feminism' and consequently feel attracted to the transgressive elements putatively offered by queer. The issues at stake were not specifically about SM practices; instead, these became the focus for a growing need to discuss desire, fantasies and sexual practices without being policed or labelled 'post-feminist'.

SM acts were, in the eyes of LASM (Lesbians Against Sadomasochism) irredeemably connected to heterosexuality. As most heterosexuality was considered violence to women, the added ritualization in SM sex made it more horrific and dangerous. In lesbian SM, the fact that the oppressor (male) wasn't actually doing it made it even more reprehensible.
Susan Ardill and Sue O'Sullivan, 'Upsetting an Applecart'

By no means all the anti-censorship lobby were SM dykes, any more than all queers are sex radicals. Yet lesbians who were pro-sex found themselves accused of being anti-feminist or even fascist, while trying to defend the right to have SM sex, without trashing 'vanilla' sex as dull and unexploratory. The reactionary, divisive dichotomy of good girl/bad girl silenced doubt and confusion, pressurising women to join one camp or the other. For women involved in SM practices, there was nowhere to express fears that their power dynamics might be slipping over into other parts of their lives or whatever, so busy were they defending their right to exist at all.

The 'Summer of Sex' of 1988 was a landmark in the pro-sex/pro-censorship debate. Despite increased repression from the right and vociferous cries of 'post-feminist libertarian' from the feminist left, there was a renewed confidence and productivity among anti-censorship lesbians. The following twelve months saw many British 'firsts':

- Thrilling Bits, the first lesbian sex toy and magazine mail-order company was established
- *Serious Pleasure*, a collection of lesbian erotic writings, and Joan Nestle's *A Restricted Country* were published by Sheba Feminist Publishers
- the first lesbian sex magazine, *Quim*, came out (even though most stockists refused to carry it...)

- a mixed conference organised by Sheba called 'Putting the Sex Back into Politics' significantly acknowledged the relevance of gay men to the lesbian anti-censorship struggle.

There was also the notorious first Lesbian Summer School. Not quite St Trinian's, but almost. A group of non-violent, anti-porn radfems physically attacked two women organisers and a video machine previewing Sheila McLaughlin's *She Must Be Seeing Things*. The film depicted two women who dared incorporate role-play into the sexual and racial dynamics of their relationship – **dynamite** to a lesbian community ready to explode with the tensions, resentments and fear that silenced curiosity and desire engender. There was an assumption that all black lesbians found SM of any kind racist, fascist and oppressive and that black lesbians involved with SM or its defence had somehow been deluded by 'bad' white lesbians. Black women were regarded as worth saving and reconverting back to the PC line, which desperately needed black women's faces in its ranks.

For the first time there was a specifically cultural, as well as sexual, site for the discussions that had been provoked by the LLGC row. Like much of the pro-sex material that pro-sex women end up being forced to defend for its ideological significance, the film was not without its flaws. But what it did was to reassert an unspoken agenda of 'difference'. At this time, as Sheila McLaughlin suggested:

Women were representing themselves to the world as each other, as like each other, looking the same. It's a re-establishing of difference, which re-establishes a certain eroticism in relationships. I wanted to bring out the aggression in their sex, to show that the eroticism that's there is not just 'nice'. 'Screen', Vol 28, No 4, Autumn 1987

Here was a film showing a lesbian, inter-racial couple who enjoyed SM sex, talked about 'cocks', and socialised and worked with 'the enemy'. In one scene, Agatha, tormented by her suspicions that her lover, Jo, is having an affair with a man, dresses in a suit and visits a shop to buy a dildo.

Agatha dressing as a man masquerades as that which she is threatened by. In a way, she is using the disguise to do battle with the thing that she is disguised as. By representing herself in the image of the rival, she deflates it.
Sheila McLaughlin, ibid.

By positing an **active** desire between **women** that was not characterised as masculine in its sex scenes, the film challenged the idea that voyeurism is male and therefore necessarily exploitative. (When Jo asks Agatha, 'Do you really want a cock?', she replies, 'No, yes, maybe, sometimes, but I don't want to be a man.') And there were scenes showing Agatha's violent, jealous fantasies of her 'unfaithful' lover's death or mutilation. Interestingly enough, however, the film was never marketed as a lesbian SM film, and indeed those who went to see it as such were bitterly disappointed.

Yet the response from some of the lesbians who first saw the film was astonishing. There seemed to be an inability to distinguish fantasy from action within the narrative, let alone any willingness to engage in a debate about uncomfortable aspects of fantasy itself: the fantasies we have that we may not like, or which arouse us in spite of their lack of political correctness. Some women, going on the film's reputation alone, set up a 'Porn-Free Zone' outside the screening room in an attempt to intimidate and 'rescue' those who were going in. The following article demonstrates the moral high-ground of this position in its tone of a judge summing up to deliver a verdict of guilty. I waited for the black cross on my front door.

One lesbian said that the images in the film – of women being degraded, fucked by men, anti-lesbian images, the lesbian dressed as a man in the sex shop buying a penis [sic] – override any erotic glances between the two women. Another lesbian pointed out that lesbian feminists have been discussing our fantasies for years and don't need to glorify them on the screen. A lesbian commented after the film that Inge Blackman and Cherry Smyth [we both presented the film and struggled to chair a discussion] were trying to create a SM dynamic which left many lesbians distressed and crying. 'The Lesbian Information Service Newsletter', August 1988

Many younger lesbians who hadn't anticipated the tone of the event arrived wearing lipstick and were told that they obviously weren't 'real' lesbians. One wrote to the organisers afterwards:

Before coming to the Summer School, I called myself a lesbian feminist. But over the past four days I felt more and more outcast because of my political beliefs. I was told yesterday I must be an SM dyke for thinking the way I do, and today, that I was 'a lesbian from the waist downwards'. I really resent this kind of labelling and patronisation from older lesbians which closed off discussion between the two 'factions'.

The sexual slur is particularly pertinent to a discussion of queer, where a similar voice can be heard, asking queers to tone down the sexual element, the sexual upfrontness, the 'Queer as Fuck' T-shirts. The explicitness is seen as treacherous, as is the use of the word 'queer' itself.

The following year a series of lesbian workshops called 'Making It Public' was created to discuss inter-racial relationships, taboos, butch-femme, monogamy, non-monogamy, disability and sex, safer sex and sex toys. There was an attempt inspired by the Barnard Conference on female sexuality (see *Pleasure and Danger: Exploring Female Sexuality*) to secure an atmosphere that would be non-judgemental and would avoid the SM/vanilla chasm. There was a tremendous feeling of release, relief, excitement, recognition, fear and energy which could well be dubbed 'queer' by those who use the term to describe breaking down boundaries and transgressing moral and social codes. The 'Sexual Taboos' workshop revealed the diversity of the sexual practices and fears which had yet to be addressed by lesbian feminism:

I want to totally overpower someone/ To be paid well by a rich dyke to be her toy girl/ Wanking with a gay man, being fucked by a stranger/ I want to piss in my lover's face/ Fucking my mother while my father is watching/ I would like to be fucked by a woman with a dildo/ Be part of a gang bang with men/ I want my lover to fantasise that she's making me pregnant when we fuck with our dildo/ Tying my lover up and beating her. I will not do this because I do not trust how much this is patri-sexually constructed desire/ I like to look and feel sexy/ I want to have a sexual relationship with a number of women at the same time and not feel guilty/ To rape a woman/ My father is fucking my brother. I am fucking my mother. My sister is watching/ To wear a skirt/ I would like to fuck nice-looking boys and not fuck up my identity as a lesbian/ To be raped/ I want to fuck a gay man in the ass with a dildo/ I do sometimes find women who wear make-up, pretty dresses etc, very attractive. I'm told this is wrong – why?/ I'd like to fuck another woman in front of my lover/ Watching sexually explicit films/ I'd like to have sex with my dog

The amount of trust necessary to enable each and every one of these statements to be risked was both empowering and liberating. Although about a quarter of the women who attended were black or Asian lesbians, there was still not enough trust to speak about issues of race in the 'Sexual Taboos' workshop. The session on 'Racial Taboos' was more highly charged and showed how little white lesbians had begun to address issues of race:

I'd be scared if I fancied a black woman that the attraction would be for the wrong reasons, eg because she is black, and 'exotic'/ I would not allow my white lover to tie me down when we're making love, but I feel OK about tying her down because I'm subjugated by white people all the time/ My awareness of racial issues has only come of age as I am now with a black lover. In a relationship when both are white, tunnel vision ensues – I would be hesitant to approach a black woman in a club/ As a white woman I am nearly always conscious of the blackness of the black women I mix with – and some of the time of my whiteness/ My taboo is never relating to a black women sexually again, for fear of cancelling her out. But I'm not happy with this/ I feel tired of other black women not being supportive of me and ignoring my white lover/ I wonder if my lover wants to disown me because I'm white/ Feeling as if white women who have lots of relationships with Afro-Caribbean women view Asian women as wimpy, sexually femmy, submissive etc/ I hate the reverent way race is discussed – I hate the fear – my own – of being accused of anything. I'm proud to be a coconut/ As a white woman I find that white women sometimes overcompensate in their acknowledgement of my black lover which creates difficulties in my relationship with her/ Being seen as white, which I'm not, and feeling that I'm not taken seriously/ I want to be fully accepted by my Jewish lover's family...

If queer is going to make lasting and significant changes, it must not assume that all transgressions happen on a sexual level. For many white and black lesbians and gay men, having an inter-racial relationship is still intrinsically transgressive. How can queer help us to deal with anti-semitism and racism on the scene? Will it help provide us with ways of tackling homophobia in our own communities?

Learning from the boys

The 'Making It Public' series came too early to discuss what was to become one of the most vital, engaging aspects of queer politics for dykes: working with gay men, gaining an understanding of and appropriating their sexual culture. Radfems such as Sheila Jeffreys have argued that lesbian sex has been corrupted by gay male sexual practice and even discouraged dykes from giving support to the Operation Spanner campaign on the grounds that they 'did not approve of gay sexual abuse'. The fear of admitting to having, or desiring to have, 'politically incorrect' sex has not only inhibited lesbians from talking to each other, but strengthened the barriers between lesbians and gay men.

Ann mustered up all her courage and said,
'I have a cock.'
'You look pretty good for a mid op,' he said.
His name was Mike.
'No. I'm not a transsexual. I'm a lesbian with a penis. I know this is unusual,
but would you like to suck my cock?'
Ann had always wanted to say 'suck my cock' because it was one thing a lot
of people said to her and she never said it to anyone.
Sarah Schulman in 'Women on Women', ed. J. Nestle and N. Holoch

In the past two years more lesbians have been discussing their erotic responses to gay male pornography and incorporating gay male sexual iconography into their fantasies, sex play and cultural representations. The language of gay male sex and the public spaces for its enactment are more developed and specific and have no doubt increased the articulateness of lesbian sexual expression. There is a growing lesbian and gay alliance which seems to work across much more fluid boundaries, definitions and self-understandings. It began to happen before the recent coinage of the term 'queer', but is part of what allowed queer to happen when and how it did. Gay male sexual practices and identities were being radically altered by AIDS, with less focus on penetration and on who penetrates whom, resulting in a more interchangeable active/passive pattern. Meanwhile, dykes who had reclaimed butch-femme identifications were now shifting their sources. Unlike the butch-femme dynamic which borrows from the heterosexual model, the butch daddy dyke and lesbian boy, for example, appropriate masculine codes without denying the femaleness of their protagonists. While there remain vestiges of mutual caution, a fear on both sides of exposing ignorance (from 'Oh I've never heard of G-spot ejaculations! Do all women have them?'

to 'So your piles improve when you get fucked more up the ass?') and a cautious denial of the erotic charge of otherness, the openness and willingness between lesbians and gay men to share experiences and learn from each other is refreshing the parts an accusatory feminism and misogynist separatism could not reach.

Della Grace's photograph, 'Lesbian Cock', presents two lesbians dressed in leather and biker caps, both sporting moustaches and one holding a lifelike dildo protruding from her crotch. In this delicious parody of phallic power, laced with an envy few feminists feel able to admit, these women are strong enough to show they're women. Their pose encapsulates their desire for the upfront cruising style, the eroticisation of the ass, casual sex, cottaging, penetration and the economic power and social privilege of the gay male.

Now some of us are more confident and able to play with notions of gender. We are not afraid that if we use a dildo we are aping heterosexual sex. We have permission to exchange power. Sex is not a pretty act – always sweet, tender, comfortable or understandable. We are all animals, very basic and raw. But it makes people uncomfortable to be reminded of that. We want to be civilised. Della Grace

Unlike Agatha in *She Must Be Seeing Things*, who takes on a **heterosexual** male disguise in order to deflate it and rob it of its power, these women are playing out and exaggerating their fascination with the sexual power of the gay male stereotype. It is a stereotype taken beyond its expected limits and framed by a knowledge of the danger the image represents, not only to the radical feminist but also to homophobic culture. These women are lesbian enough to risk the double-edged sword. There is also a tease towards the gay male voyeur in the pose which says, 'Hey Daddy, almost fooled ya! See here, your look isn't so very macho, so very transgressive, for we can take it further'. The image boasts of the fun of a butch-on-butch dyke camp style that doesn't need to bind its breasts to impress. The gay man in return admires the butch's assumed masculinity, fetishistically packed in leather.

When I cruise gay men as a boy, I know full well that I have to stay as a boy the whole time... I lick Daddy's boots and suck his cock and get on my face for him, raise my ass up at the first brush of his cock on my cheeks. I beg daddy to fuck my ass and I promise I'll be his good boy always. I love being the boy, but I don't like having to be two people to get what I want. I really want the men I fuck to turn me over and see the whole me: the woman in the boy, the boy in the woman. Carol Queen in 'Taste of Latex'

Lesbian 'maleness' may be a 'gay maleness' – not a re-enactment of fixed gender roles, but an exploration of the very signs 'male' and 'female'.
Julia Creet, 'Outlook', Winter 1991

Are lesbians reasserting, rather than subverting, a dominant male sexuality? Do lesbians have to appropriate phallocentric images of sexuality in order to represent an active sexual arousal and autonomy because there is no such obvious symbol in lesbian sex?

Lesbian feminists think things like lesbians giving blow-jobs to dildos should be kept quiet. Gender play is curious. It's been OK for years for gay men to play at being women, or for one partner to act the part, but for women to indulge in gender-fuck somehow isn't acceptable. But lesbians do. Lesbians even have 'gay male sex'. Della Grace

Della Grace insists that the iconography and dynamics she employs are not 'male', but rather 'butch' or 'fetish'. Some of the iconography is indeed robbed from women sex-trade workers and post-punk fashion, which injects a violent autonomy into femme chic, making it trashy and threatening, rather than vulnerable and submissive, to wear a mini-skirt and revealing bodice. The supremo exponent of this style of trash power is Madonna herself, who is probably one of the most famous examples of queer transgression. The femme in some of Della's photographic scenarios works across hetero and homo definitions and gender boundaries: she is a straight women fucking a gay/straight man; a lesbian fucking a lesbian dressed as a gay man; a lesbian dressed as a straight women fucking a lesbian.

I would argue that what is happening is not a simple mapping of gay male sexuality on to the lesbian body, but a practice that relies heavily on self-conscious parody. It is constituted as queer at that level. However, when lesbians take on behaviour perceived as macho and beat up their femme or lesbian boy-identified lovers in the name of transgression, then it's plain old reactionary chickenshit.

Domination or dialogue?

The new separation between sexual practice and sexual identity is allowing lesbians to expand our practice, to question the fixedness of our identities and to invent new metaphors for sexual pleasure that can embrace wider interpretations of sex and gender. But if lesbians can empathise with, imitate and reflect gay male sexual culture, is there a similar appropriation of lesbian practices by gay men? Do gay men fetishise the cunt and breasts or learn from dykes how to acknowledge and parody their femininity?

On the whole, there seems to be little reciprocity: no doubt because of the relative lack of sexual and social power to which women have access. If dykes assume daddy/boy codes, they are mirroring a powerful aesthetic of masculinity; when gay men reflect back mummy/girl codes (which have no fetishised sexual purchase as yet, even for dykes), you have camp or full-blown drag, which is almost always a parody of, or homage to, **heterosexual** femininity. It is a tradition that is as old as queer in its first usage.

When the GLF began in the 1970s, drag was always seen as an integral part of both gay culture and activism, but gradually a new class of professional homosexuals developed who looked down on drag queens as figures who somehow fulfilled a stereotype. Between them and the radical feminists, who thought drag was degrading to women, the whole concept of drag became marginalised and pushed into the background. Julian Hows, Sister of Perpetual Indulgence, From Drags to Bitches, 'Him', January 1992

Drag has always been the most visual way of expressing your queerness. It says you're not interested in being tolerated if the price is to succumb to some dreary conformity. Drag takes you beyond the macho posturing of suits and ties... It allows you to explore your own fantasies and to confront the conventions that control us sexually and emotionally. Patrick McCann, from the WIG (Work It Girl) OutRage affinity group, ibid

Yet gay men do find an erotic charge in images of lesbians parodying their own sexual codes, as witnessed by a review of Della Grace's book, *Love Bites.*

Pictured are two figures dressed in leather... the erotic signifiers would not be out of place in a photo by Mapplethorpe or a drawing by Tom of Finland... The difference is that the photographer and models acting out the fantasy are lesbians. I want to talk about how I'm turned on by this photograph, but I'm wondering whether I even have the right and assuming I do, whether anyone is going to listen. Paul Burston, 'Capital Gay', 21 June 1991

The article received two letters from women, one insisting that she wasn't going to have a gay man tell her what to think, the other contesting the fact that lesbians 'learnt' all they know about sex from gay men. While Burston's piece asserted neither, he was disappointed that it got no response from men. Gay men did approach him later and say that they appreciated his 'brave' article as it echoed their own feelings, but that they didn't want their names in print. The slur of 'bisexual' still has a firm hold, and Burston admitted to feeling anxious about the possibility of being ostracised because of what he had written.

I find macho and irony erotic, which is what I like about Della's work – not reading the women as men, but enjoying the fetish of it, as opposed to the biological body of a woman. If I fantasise about having sex with a dyke it's different than fantasising about a straight woman. Paul Burston

Transgression for its own sake?

While some women see queer as having liberated their sexual practice and others argue that it has not given them permission to do anything they would not otherwise have done, there is also a suggestion that queer will simply engender a situation where people are being transgressive for transgression's sake.

For queer, any transgression is seen as automatically radical – this so-called blurring of boundaries. It seems similar to the bohemian lifestyle of the hip set of the 20s. Dykes can talk about fucking gay or straight men. Great! Straight people think that's what we do anyway (especially the men, because they think they're too important to be excluded). It's only shocking and transgressive to hardline feminists. As long as people who are having homosexual relations have to hide, then all this blurring and transgression ain't worth shit. Inge Blackman

How queer is it if you've got a man being fucked in a public scene without a condom? Clearly it's transgressive, but it's not queer. It's reactionary and stupid and potentially lethal. Queer offers the terms of transgressive and subversive, but transgressive of what? Subversive of what? Those elements seem unsaid, lost in this wave of energy that is being named queer, but clearly has lots of other sources. Philip Derbyshire

An avant-garde and/or bohemian stance is no guarantee of 'progressive' politics, and both are primarily rebellious reactions against bourgeois conformist norms. Nor is transgression per se radical. Historically it has been linked with fascism as well as left wing politics or is perhaps more likely to lead to an apolitical dandyism. Elizabeth Wilson

It's important that nobody starts saying, 'You're not queer because you're not into leather and don't fuck in a harness'. There is that sense of reifying sexual acts above the theory. Tori Smith

People should remember that although the element of desire is an important motivation for queer culture, it's not just about sex. It's also because the mainstream public and press want to look at the sexual above all else. Tessa Boffin

Though for many lesbians, the sexually transgressive adventure had already begun before queer arrived in the late 80s, and some would argue that lesbians invented queer in the first place, the transgressive aesthetic which may be called 'queer' has given some lesbian artists a new freedom to express their lifestyles, fantasies and fears beyond the limits of homophobic conventions and the feminist ghetto. The lesbian sexual subject is born, whether she calls herself queer or not. Not only does she challenge the homo-hetero duality, she deconstructs both gender and sexuality in ways recent feminism rarely allowed and perhaps queer has not yet imagined.

No art in heaven

❢ *People have found it necessary to define their sexuality in images, in photographs and drawings and movies in order not to disappear... I'm beginning to believe that the last frontier left for radical gesture is the imagination.*❢
David Wojnarowicz, 'Close to The Knives'

❢ *Forced to define itself against the prevailing negative definitions, homosexuality has found more and more to say about love, gender and desire, while the media are burying heterosexuality in an overkill of tired tabloid clichés.*❢
Elizabeth Wilson, 'New Statesman & Society', 2 November 1990

❢ *Queer art is anything that makes heterosexuality strange and undermines it. Some heterosexual art is queer. It's less monolithic than feminist art.*❢ Isling Mack-Nataf

In the US, and to a lesser extent in Britain, there are signs of the beginnings of a queer aesthetic which has developed out of AIDS activism, anti-censorship debates, sex-positive assertion and anti-homophobic strategies. Is it address, audience, style or identity that defines queer art, or all of the above? Lesbian and gay culture was perceived by some as having reached a stalemate thanks to enforced political correctness and the tyranny of positive images. Whether queer art will replace lesbian and gay art or be purloined by commercial art and 'mainstream' publishers, cinemas, galleries and theatres, remains to be seen. But the signs so far are that it is clever enough to be cautious of being co-opted. No sooner does the establishment think it has defined 'queer' than the artists change the goalposts. In 1988, when the first ACT UP art activist group, Gran Fury, got a funded commission, it refused to dilute its irony and powerful presence. Instead, the first poster lambasted the complacency of the art world:

'WITH 42,000 DEAD, ART IS NOT ENOUGH'

Queer culture posits itself as a counter-culture to the counter-culture. Rej-

ecting the conventional boundaries and contexts of art and defying traditional evaluations, it does not claim to be eternal and truthful, but rather
temporary and tactical... But wait a minute, this all sounds like a manifesto
for feminist or spray-paint artists... But queer culture has the arrogance of
adolescence, the wisdom of knowing that fucking can be lethal and the
courage to try to assert a new dignity in the face of the AIDS crisis and
increased erasure. Born out of anger at the ways AIDS was being represented
and understood, it is fuelled by the urgency and despair of a community that
is learning about mortality first hand and fast.

Now we think
as we fuck
this nut might kill.
His kiss could turn
to stone.
Essex Hemphill, 'Conditions'

Gay men were just beginning to celebrate the body; now we have to be
more aware of the body. Dealing with sickness and mortality takes away
the idea of being respectable. Isaac Julien

Queer art rejects the need to be accepted on heterosexist terms. It is
irreverent where much lesbian and gay art was coy, shameless where some
lesbian and gay culture was apologetic. Channel Four's 'OUT' television series
may be an important and unprecedented gay intervention into mainstream
TV, but it could never be called 'queer art', for in style and address it seeks
to be tasteful and tolerated. *Longtime Companion* (Norman Rene, US,1990)
is a 'gay' film; *Poison* (Todd Haynes, US, 1991) is a 'queer' film.

At its most successful, queer art represents a vigorous challenge to the
normalisation of positive images and a radical recognition of pluralities, in
a style that flaunts conventions. At its worst, it is the shock tactics of a new
generation of lesbians and gays who, in transcending the old categories of
sexuality and gender, ignore issues of sexual inequality, class and race.

Empty frames

Cultural activism is viewed with some suspicion in this island of anti-
intellectualism, where there is little regard for artists at the best of times. Gay
or lesbian militant artists have had a tough time gaining public or private
funding; the right's rush to protect its family from contagion and hide its
terror of the body has manifested itself in rigorous censorship of any art
which challenges the enforcement of normative heterosexuality. Several local
authorities have used Clause 28 to legitimise the banning of films, poetry
readings and exhibitions. (As cited above, the 1989 'Ecstatic Antibodies:
Resisting the AIDS Mythology' show was cancelled in Salford on the grounds
that the work was pornographic and unsuitable for a 'family gallery'.) In the

US, censorship has included the 1990 defunding by the NEA (National Endowment for the Arts) of four New York performance artists who refused to sign a clause which guaranteed that they would not use the grant to depict: 'sadomasochism, homoeroticism, the sexual exploitation of children, or individuals engaged in sex acts.'

I went into a museum but they had taken down all the art. Only the empty frames were left...The guards had nothing to guard... Toilets were locked up in museums because people might think someone peeing is art... In the empty frames were the reasons why art was confiscated.
Jasper Johns – for desecrating the flag
Michelangelo – for being a homosexual
Mary Cassatt – for painting nude children... Karen Finley (NEA defunded artist) in 'High Risk', ed. A. Scholder and I. Silverberg

But censorship from the right is not the only problem. Several artists have also been disappointed by the neglect and trivialisation of art by the left. And feminist ideology created its own proscriptive agenda, which in many cases amounted to an equally rigorous form of censorship.

Art, culture and sexuality aren't considered worthy of defence by the American Left, while the Right considers art and sexuality worthy of oppression. Where was Andrea Dworkin when I was censored for doing a feminist pro-sex show? Some of what poses as feminist art is really internalised homophobia, erotophobia and fear of our bodies.
Holly Hughes, 'Capital Gay', 18 October 1991

Feminist art stinks because it is so dishonest. Feminism has often been allowed to stifle women's creativity and kept us back. We're still in an infancy of self-discovery. I have no idea what queer art is. To me, Della Grace's work is lesbian or 'woman'. It's challenging because she makes no assumptions about what a woman or lesbian is, or can be.
Inge Blackman

Inventing the lesbian

Where does the black or white lesbian queer artist appear in the British queer cultural renaissance? Does she still need to be invented? In January 1991, eighteen leading actors, directors and dramatists wrote to the *Guardian* in protest at 'queer artist' Derek Jarman's denouncement of Ian McKellen's acceptance of a knighthood. Only three dykes were prepared to be on the list of signatories, even though this was clearly an assimilationist, 'safe' intervention. How much more difficult is it for women to be out as queer artists?

Even lesbians are saying we don't exist! Lesbians are just not being invented. I think lesbians invented camp. Natalie Barney invented

salons, but when the histories are told we get written out. My answer is aesthetics – artists like Della Grace and Sarah Schulman who are inventing the lesbian and doing very serious political work – and that's why I'm in theatre. In 1984 in Toronto, a bunch of us sat round and tried to think of a word that could include the people who were disenfranchised. We founded Buddies in Bad Times Theater Company. Sue Golding

I've never described myself as a queer artist. Queer sounds contrived to me. I'm a lesbian and an artist. My work's about my sexuality but it's about my class as well. Nearly everyone's white, male and middle class. I feel marooned. I've had work sent back from right-on galleries saying they thought it could be misinterpreted. I said, 'What you're really worried about is that it's not polite, symbolic sex. You're censoring my experience'. Mandy McCartin

I've gained a lot of energy from the queer aesthetic. I want to impassion people, make them angry and shake up their complacency. I want to negotiate sexual explicitness – like how do you represent the female orgasm in film? – and show some of the problems between black and white lesbians. The characters can be irreverent in a way identity politics wouldn't allow. Isling Mack-Nataf

For women, being 'nice girls' has often been a survival strategy, but that 'safety' traps and silences us. For lesbians, invisibility has been our safety and our trap. In the face of growing threats, we refuse to be invisible nice girls any more. Susan Stewart et al, 'Drawing the Line'

While both queer men and women artists focus on the right to own and express desire, the work of dykes tends to concentrate more noticeably on sexual explicitness and exploration. White gay men have been more free to produce sexually explicit art previously and so can move on to different, some would argue broader, representations and interventions. Derek Jarman's recent film, *Edward II*, for instance, is queer not only because of its representations of homosexual sex, but because it promotes and documents queer direct action politics through its images of OutRage activists.

But a queer artist does not only create queer art. For example, Isaac Julien's *Looking For Langston* (1988) is arguably 'more queer' than his *Young Soul Rebels* (1991). The questions of audience and identity reveal themselves as more problematic for white lesbians and black lesbians and gay men than for the white gay male.

Young Soul Rebels was a queer intervention into a straight black audience. Gay men may have more pleasure from *Looking For Langston*, but there is a cosy self-referentiality in talking to ourselves. I believe in a hybrid that isn't exclusively queer, yet I do want to make very uncompromised work that totally addresses a queer audience, but always addresses a black audience as well. Isaac Julien

One of the queerest things I've seen is Paris Is Burning *(Jennie Livingstone, US, 1990). It's all about the black gay vogueing scene and can teach us more than anything about queer, because what they're doing is about survival and exploiting every economic and social system. They parody everything about the white, straight, capitalist world.* Tori Smith

I see it as part of a coming of age, a renewed confidence in the lesbian and gay communities to move on and away from purely oppositional aesthetics, in a similar way that the black communities have done here. It's about finding a space to create work artistically that can incorporate our different experiences without having to take racism, or heterosexism, as a reference point. Pratibha Parmar

One of the cultural practices in which lesbians have made the most visible intervention is photography. With Della Grace's *Love Bites* and Tessa Boffin and Jean Fraser's *Stolen Glances: Lesbians Take Photographs,* there is evidence of a distinct distancing from an essentialist lesbian sensibility. Both deconstruct the idealising, normative image of the lesbian.

Our imagination was caught by the inventiveness of lesbian photographers who had 'stolen' and inverted the meanings of heterosexual imagery... Rather than attempting to naturalise a 'lesbian aesthetic', we looked for work which concentrated on constructed, staged or self-consciously manipulated imagery which might mirror the socially constructed nature of sexuality. Tessa Boffin and Jean Fraser, 'Stolen Glances'

We didn't call it queer at the time, but looking back on it that's what it was. Gay men's reaction to the book has been interesting. In gay men's culture they have a limited repertoire of representations – pin-ups basically – and men have found the range of analysis fascinating. Tessa Boffin

Even without wearing queer hearts on their sleeves, lesbian artists have explored sexual and racial identities in what could in retrospect be claimed as queer work. For example, Tessa Boffin's 'Angelic Rebels' piece was an early representation of lesbian safer sex that attempted to construct a metaphoric approach to the charge, often made by other lesbians, that lesbians are as likely to get AIDS as nuns are.

Such women see us as nun-like in that we are an exclusive community that does not count ex-heterosexuals, bisexuals, IV-drug users or prostitutes among its members... This view fails to acknowledge there are certain activities: rimming, fisting, cunnilingus, and so on, which cut across the fragile boundaries of sexual orientation, and could put anyone, regardless of their sexuality or gender, at risk. Tessa Boffin, 'Ecstatic Antibodies'

One of the black lesbian photographers in *Stolen Glances,* Ingrid Pollard, was able to come out for the first time in a self-portrait in the book because she felt the context made the process safer. Her series of images and texts, entitled 'Deny: Imagine: Attack' examines the choices we are presented with.

Image One, DENY: a black woman shields her face with the back of her hand as if from a slap, the light of truth, the shame.

Image Two, IMAGINE: fragments of a black woman's naked body undercut the text, 'Butch – a very pronounced tendency among sexually inverted women to adopt male attire... Femme – when they still retain female garments these show traits of masculine simplicity...'(Havelock Ellis)

Image Three, ATTACK: 'Sticks and stones will... bent, manhater, bulldagger, lezzie, queer...' is intercut with images of a black woman holding a bamboo rod, caressing a smooth white stone and touching a garland of flowers. The sense of calmness and strength, of self-protection and dignity draws out the paradox at the heart of the piece – that the words DO hurt as much as stones, and we ARE attacked with sticks.

Mumtaz Karimjee also uses self-portraits and text to explore the ground between the myths of lesbianism as 'The eastern disease' and 'The western disease'. The text, describing tribadism as a savage, uncivilised practice only 'dirty' eastern women could indulge in, is juxtaposed with an image of Karimjee staring at her mirror-image:

'The Moslem Harem is a great school for this "Lesbian (which I call Atossan) love"; these tribades are mostly known by peculiarities of form and features, hairy cheeks and upper lips, gruff voices, hircine odour and the large projecting clitoris with erectile powers.'

This is juxtaposed with another image which shows Karimjee looking at an Asian newspaper headline which reads, 'Urmila weds Leela, both get sacked'. 'Stolen Glances', ed. T. Boffin and J. Fraser

Where do I locate myself in the 'we's' and 'us'es' that I've invoked so far, when I don't find that these pluralities fully embrace my black lesbian self? How can I, when both the lesbian and the gay male communities figure race in such disparate ways? Dykes politicise it, gay men eroticise it, either perception effectively neutralising any middle ground on which I can stand and say my piece. Jackie Goldsby, 'Stolen Glances', ed. T. Boffin and J. Fraser

There are the beginnings of a transcendent, inclusive culture, but not transcendent or inclusive enough. Even the much lauded art activist group, Gran Fury, became a men-only group with one token black member.

I was a member of 'Art Positive' – an affinity group of ACT UP, New York – we were concerned with a multi-racial, multi-sexual artists' response. Art Positive got less press. Even though I love those white boys in Gran Fury (they put me on their 'Greed and Indifference Kills' poster and 'Read My Lips' T-shirt) they were really closed. It's hard for me to criticise them because 98 per cent of the people who buy my photos are white boys. But I did have a problem that they didn't accept a few people of color into their group. So Art Positive sprung up and we did posters and T-shirts which said: 'AIDS IS KILLING ART AND NOW HOMOPHOBIA IS KILLING ARTISTS'. Lola Flash

While the US has produced several artists who could be called 'queer' – from performance artists Split Britches, Annie Sprinkle, Holly Hughes and Karen Finley, to the eighteen-year-old dyke video artist Sadie Benning, whose *Portrait of the Artist as a Young Dyke* has yet to reach these shores – ask any British dyke to name a queer artist and she will more than likely ask, 'what do you mean by queer?' Then she may suggest Derek Jarman, Della Grace or Neil Bartlett. Ask Jarman why there are still no lesbian characters in his films and he will tell you:

It is time I used more dykes and black people and I was aware of this from the very beginning, but somehow where my films were pushed made it difficult. Derek Jarman

Ask Della whether she calls herself a queer artist and she will reply:

I had my photos in a queer culture exhibition in Toronto and I can relate to queer culture in a large sense, but I see it as a discussion that a lot of people aren't ready to have. I don't think of myself as queer. Della Grace

For me, queer has given a name to the text I have been compelled to write to legitimise my life, to articulate my lifestyle and to resist my destiny. It made me bold and unrepentant, inspired by Dorothy Allison, Joan Nestle, Sarah Schulman, Jane DeLynn, Cheryl Clarke, Jewelle Gomez and many more:

I am a professional lady –
Acceptable;
I am a predatory pervert –
Shocking;
Efficient, disruptive, reliable, abnormal –
I introduce clients,
I seduce women.
My lover knows hard wisdom
Learnt from silences in public,
Where unsettled voices
Piss abuse –
'What d'ya call that, mate?
Is it a girl, or a geezer?'
'At times like this,' she says,
'I wish I had a submachine gun.'
I watch my quiet and beautiful terrorist
Despised, pick herself up
Become a woman again.

Our private love trembles to be enough
Where no rituals reward our desire;
Shy and weary we battle
For how we are
And map out shorter, safer routes
Through forbidden territories
Which grow large,
More dangerous.
From 'Private Love', Cherry Smyth, 1990

In the morning my lover has tea with her mother. I am in her little girl's bed, the daughter's bed, the baby sister's bed. This gives me a delicious frisson to be so near her past, her childhood when she still believed she was a boy. I pretend to be asleep. I wish I was invisible or had a huge cock between my legs. Why is it so hard to be welcomed, to be 'just what they wanted' for their little Beth Ann? No matter how charming, how polite, friendly, feminine or masculine I am, I will never be good enough, for I am not a man.

On the wall is a framed family tree that stretches back four generations. The Daidones, the Johnsons, the Prestias, the Spinellis, the Caferellis, the Morrisons, the McDonalds, the Damms. Everyone is married off, has been given a branch, but my lover. The tree stops with her. I want to give her a baby now. I want her to have hers now. I want to be on that tree. I hate that tree and want to sabotage it for I know its branches will never extend to us... Cherry Smyth, August 1991

Towards a queer planet

> ❢ *It's time to put our cocks and cunts on the line, to smash once and for all the lie that we're all the same, that we want to be like the gay and straight zombies out there who watch propaganda TV, who believe the lies in the Sun and the Guardian, who think they've a right to judge us, our bodies, our lovers, our lives... It's time to smash the myth of the "gay" community which allows fools like Stonewall and Capital Gay to sell us out, to sell our souls to the devils of straight culture...❢*
> 'Queer Power Now', Anonymous leaflet, London 1991

> ❢ *OutRage has become an institution. It's almost part of the Establishment it set out to destabilise. But OutRage the organisation has become far less important than OutRage the ideology, to the point where it wouldn't really matter if the organisation went under.❢*
> Chris Woods, 'Independent on Sunday', 10 November 1991

> ❢ *Even when coupled with a toleration of minority sexualities, heteronormativity has a totalising tendency that can only be overcome by actively imagining a necessarily and desirably queer world.❢* Michael Warner, 'Fear of a Queer Planet'

The rise of queer politics in Britain has created a false division between the good and the bad gays, with the government choosing to legitimise the Stonewall Group as 'representative' and shun OutRage as 'irrational'. Among lesbians and gays themselves, opinion is split between those who insist queer activism is 'too extreme', and those who appreciate OutRage's continued success in promoting a political agenda and pushing gay and lesbian issues on to the mainstream news in a way former lesbian and gay politics had failed to do. For example, the biggest public march by lesbians and gays, Gay Pride, is not yet assured mainstream news coverage, and in any case has become less a political statement, more a piss-up in the park.

I keep going to OutRage because it has continually got the word gay

into the news. It still functions in terms of putting the queer agenda into lesbian and gay politics and putting gay politics into the straight community. Tori Smith

In Britain, as both main parties move towards the centre, Ian McKellen (of the Stonewall Group) has had tea with John Major – a major symbolic event, unthinkable under Thatcher, but actually unthinkable under any previous Labour Prime Minister as well. There's going to be a normalising discourse. We'll probably see the age of consent brought into line with European Law. Simon Watney, 'frieze', Issue 2, 1991

With the development of a new European identity for Britain, will queer politics retain its relevance as an agency for social change? As things stand, there is no 'European Law' as yet on the age of consent, but there is a general consensus that the age of consent for homosexuals should be equal to that for heterosexuals, at either fifteen or sixteen. A majority of European countries have an equal age of consent, from twelve years old in Spain and the Netherlands to sixteen in Belgium, Norway, Switzerland, Portugal and the Ukraine. Britain has the highest age of consent for gay men in Europe (twenty-one).

The European Social Charter's human rights clause does not yet extend to lesbian and gay rights. And as yet, Britain has not adopted the EC code of practice on homosexuality and boasts the most oppressive anti-homosexual legislation in Europe. Homosexuality is still **illegal** on the Isle of Man, despite the fact that the island's outdated laws break the European Code on Human Rights. Meanwhile, Europe is experiencing the most intense rise in racism for fifty years, with growing attacks on black and minority communities, growing success at the polls for extreme right and nationalist political parties, and more stringent restrictions on immigration and asylum rights. Such a climate can only lead to increased homophobia, with increased curbs on the movement of people who are HIV positive or have AIDS. The British National Party's latest stickers include 'For Family, For God, For Nation' and 'Fight AIDS – outlaw homosexuality'.

With its anti-assimilationist stance, can the queer agenda help to achieve constitutional reform in Britain? Some well-intentioned activists have insisted that it is divisive and meaningless merely to campaign for lesbian and gay sexual rights within a system that can sentence people above the age of consent for consensual sex carried out in private, as in the Operation Spanner or Jennifer Saunders cases. They argue that the law should be expanded to protect a wider interpretation of 'deviancy'.

Concepts of sexual orientation, of gender preference, must be replaced with a new model which acknowledges sexual diversity across perceived boundaries. Unless we can move sex rights... into an exploration of how the individual can be guaranteed sex freedoms around choice and consent, then we're wasting our time. Chris Woods, 'Gay Times', December 1991

It seems utopian to suggest that the law could be reformed to serve such a broad constituency. As the porn wars have shown, terms such as 'degrading' and 'obscene' can be interpreted very differently, and it seems difficult to imagine that terms like 'choice' and 'consent' will cease to be used to serve the subjective needs of the hetero-patriarchy. I would argue that as long as the dominant ideology needs to create a demonised 'other', it will manipulate legislation to punish the 'deviant'.

Post-queer

While social and cultural pressures on lesbian and gay politics and the shape of the AIDS epidemic are very different in the US and Britain, the lesbian and gay movement here has always been influenced by US developments and directions. The situation in the US at present seems to be heading towards a post-queer position in which a new militancy is finding a loud and exigent expression. The recognition of the privileges of reproductive sexuality, for example, has brought the rhetorical insult 'breeders' into wider use by some queers to define heterosexuals. In addition to ignoring the fact that lesbians and gays also breed and parent, and that not all heterosexuals do, there is an aggressive generic separatism here which recalls the virulence of the early 'manhating' feminists and the oppressive anti-heterosexuality that often extended to women who fucked with men, were pregnant or had children. Many of us who have not fulfilled our 'reproductive destiny' no doubt empathise with the anger of the disenfranchised, but targeting 'breeders' reinforces rather than weakens the homo-hetero duality that privileges heterosexuality. It also denies the powerfully charged ambivalences towards parenting that neither the lesbian and gay 'community' nor the queer agenda seems to have addressed. Where are the crèches?

Several US cities have recently seen the birth of groups of 'New Radicals' – young queers who are too queer for Queer Nation and have begun to pit themselves in opposition, not to heterosexuals, but to the 'assimilationist', sell-out lesbian and gay 'community'.

The New Radicals accuse gays and lesbians of appeasement, of complicity in the patriarchal sexism and racism that the early gay-libbers once had a mandate to challenge. Pointing to the rampant gender and racial segregation and class discrimination in gay society, they label gays 'heterosexist' – and they mean it.
Brian Rafferty, 'NYQ', No 11, 12 January 1992

The New Radicals claim that the gay ghetto withdrew its challenges to straight society and simply replicated its privileges. But they fail to acknowledge that in many cases the ghetto was not entirely self-imposed, and that many gays and lesbians were disenfranchised within it. Issues like support, employment and housing have drawn lesbians and gays to urban ghettos as much as the counter culture and club scene, and in Britain, in any case, the ghettos are too small to operate on an opted-out basis. Although there is a growing materialist conformity, should lesbians and gays have a greater moral responsibility than heterosexuals to challenge the inequities of race, sex and class? This kind of essentialism echoes the 'claiming our own' ideology behind outing, which suggests that lesbians and gays are more aware of oppression *per se*. There are elements of post-queer which are much more frightening than queer itself and signal an attempt to dismiss and problematise former labels rather than transcend and transgress them.

We will not tolerate any form of lesbian and gay philosophy. We will not tolerate their voluntary assimilation into heterosexual culture... We will not tolerate their trivialization of racism... Furthermore if we see lesbians and gays being assaulted on the streets, we will not intervene, we will join in... Effective immediately, [we are] at war with lesbians and gays.
Bimbox, Toronto 1991

In Britain, too, there is a 'too queer to be OutRaged' group called 'Homocult-perverters of culture', based in Manchester. They declare that 'lesbian and gay' are 'poncy words' to describe:

Persils fucked up by privilege who wish to blend with sick society rather than change it... OutRage is a cosy sham. You can only be outraged by what surprises you. It's no surprise to common queers that there is no justice for us. We are not outraged. WE ARE DEFIANT.
Anonymous Homocult poster, Manchester 1991

While Homocult points out some of the inadequacies of 'lesbian and gay' identities, its divisive, anti-assimilationist stance risks comparison with the anarchist Class War rag that rages away into oblivion. It smacks of the tyranny of the anti-materialist socialists who railed against property ownership and privilege in the 70s and had mortgages by the mid-80s. It refuses to acknowledge that not all lesbians and gays are 'persils', ie whiter than white, and that for many in black, working-class or disabled 'communities', to claim the word gay is still a radical act. Is 'Lesbocult' being established as a sub-group, I wonder...?

I get angry that queer is becoming another form of political correctness. If you say you're queer, then everyone else can be shouted down. 'They're the baddies because they're lesbian and gay pinkos and we're the radical queers with attitude.' Paul Burston

For me, 'queer' has always been a refuge and I'm hesitant about what's happening to it in the US now, where it seems to be used more for positing the worst aspects of 'gay'. Sue Golding

Queer may have injected camp back into campaigning, as one activist put it, but new pluralities fail to make old oppressions redundant. Until queer politics visibilises white lesbians and black lesbians and gay men, it still privileges the experience and agendas of white gay men. There is a danger that the new essentialism will erase the strategies lesbians and gays have used to survive, in the same way as lesbian feminism refused the butch-femme identifications of 50s lesbians and the subversive particularity of camp. Queer will fail if it fails to address the relevance of identity politics.

Queer is not about fucking your lover when you have one room with your kid; queer is not about how you get off if you spend your life in a wheelchair. Even as I say this I feel a sort of prescriptive element saying, 'That's dull and moralising'. And if that's true, then we have a problem locating queer politics in anything that looks like a broader strategy for change. Philip Derbyshire

Queer is more likely to engage black gay men first and the more visible black people are in its representations and campaigns, the more attracted black women will be. Isling Mack-Nataf

Ironically, in the midst of all this activism, I rarely see gay people being openly affectionate with each other in the streets any more. Gay men are still more visible and our culture seems to be taken up with clubs, clothes and coupling. Inge Blackman

But just as the many positive-image portraits that legitimised lesbian lifestyles were powerful in their own way, some argue that new 'queer' images promise 'what is yet to be – lesbian sexuality as present, hot and inclusive'.

These images are before anything else idealising: they attempt to fix desire as iconically as formal portraits fix identity. Where scarcity existed, they propose plenitude: tattooed women, non-thin women, women of colour, physically disabled women, butch women, femme women. And this, I would argue, can only advance everyone's agendas.
Jan Zita Grover, 'Stolen Glances', ed. T. Boffin and J. Fraser

Despite reservations I and other lesbians, gay men and queers have ex-pressed, queer politics offers a radical reclamation of the past and urgent questioning of the present. Younger lesbians and gay men have come out post-Thatcher, post-Clause 28, in a climate of safer sex, of a painful awareness of our mortality and in a culture where racism and sexism are increasingly contested, yet homophobia is still condoned. Their sense of injustice and indignation has reinvented direct action that means what it says:

We will not respect your laws because your laws don't respect us.
Peter Tatchell, on a recent OutRage march on parliament to demand gay and lesbian equality

Queer culture and politics herald a lesbian and gay sexuality that is SEXUAL, SEXY and SUBVERSIVE – not only of heterosexist notions of being, but of former lesbian and gay orthodoxies. The huge wave of energy unleashed by queer politics has enabled powerful alliances between lesbians and gay men, defying the separatism of the lesbian feminist movement and the misogyny of the gay male community. In a necessary coalition to fight the increased fundamentalism, racism and homophobia and continued sexism and discrimination against people with disabilities, issues will not retain single-gender status and limitations; fear of difference will not block our right to express our desires, fantasies and ability to become sexual subjects; and gay men will acknowledge and utilise the role black and white lesbians have played in political struggles, which may well have been queer under a different name.

Queer promises a refusal to apologise or assimilate into invisibility. It provides a way of asserting desires that shatter gender identities and sexualities, in the manner some early Gay Power and lesbian feminist activists once envisaged. Perhaps it will fail to keep its promise, but its presence now in the early 90s marks the shape of the territory to come with an irrevocable and necessary passion.

Bibliography

Ardill, Susan and O'Sullivan, Sue, 'Upsetting an Applecart: Difference, Desire and Lesbian Sadomasochism, *Feminist Review*, London, No 23, Summer 1986

Bad Object Choices, eds., *How Do I Look?: Queer Film & Video*, Seattle, Bay Press, 1991

Bartlett, Neil, *Ready to Catch Him Should He Fall*, Harmondsworth, Penguin, 1992

Boffin, Tessa and Fraser, Jean, eds., *Stolen Glances: Lesbians Take Photographs*, London, Pandora Press, 1991

Boffin, Tessa and Gupta, Sunil, eds., *Ecstatic Antibodies: Resisting the AIDS Mythology*, London, Rivers Oram Press, 1990

Crimp, Douglas and Rolston, Adam, *AIDS Demo Graphics*, Seattle, Bay Press, 1990

De Lauretis, Teresa, ed., 'Queer Theory, Lesbian & Gay Sexualities', *differences*, Providence, Brown University, Vol 3, No 2, Summer 1991

DeLynn, Jane, *Don Juan in The Village*, London, Serpent's Tail, 1991

Feminist Review, 'Perverse Politics: Lesbian Issues' No 34, Spring 1990

Feminist Review, 'Pornography', No 36, Autumn 1990

Fuss, Diana, ed., *Inside/Out: Lesbian Theories, Gay Theories*, Princeton University, 1992

Grace, Della, *Love Bites*, London, Gay Men's Press, 1991

Greyson, John, Gever, Martha and Parmar, Pratibha, eds., *Queer Looks* (US, forthcoming)

Hemphill, Essex, *Brother to Brother: New Writings by Black Gay Men*, Boston, Alyson Publications, 1991

Hemphill, Essex, *Conditions*, Washington DC, Be Bop Books, 1986

Holoch, Naomi and Nestle, Joan, eds., *Women on Women: An Anthology of Lesbian Short Fiction*, New York, Plume, 1990

Jarman, Derek, *Queer Edward*, London, British Film Institute Publications, 1991

Juno, Andrea and Vale, V., eds., *Angry Women*, San Francisco, Re/Search Publications, 1991

Kosofsky Sedgwick, Eve, *The Epistemology of the Closet*, Los Angeles, University of California Press, 1990

Nestle, Joan, *A Restricted Country*, London, Sheba Feminist Publishers, 1988

Outlook, National Lesbian and Gay Quarterly, San Francisco Outlook Foundation, Nos 11 and 12, Spring and Winter 1991

Queen, Carol, 'When the Lights Changed', *Taste of Latex*, Vol 1, No 4, Winter 1990-91

Quim, London, Issue 3, Winter 1991

Rodgerson, Gillian and Wilson, Eilzabeth, eds., *Pornography and Censorship: The Case Against Censorship*, London, Lawrence and Wishart, 1991

Screen, Vol 28, No 4, Autumn 1987

Scholder, Amy and Silverberg, Ira, eds., *High Risk: An Anthology of Forbidden Writings*, London, Serpent's Tail, 1991

Serious Pleasure – Lesbian Erotic Stories and Poetry, London, Sheba Feminist Publishers, 1989

More Serious Pleasure – Lesbian Erotic Stories and Poetry, London, Sheba Feminist Publishers, 1990

Showalter, Elaine, *Sexual Anarchy*, London, Bloomsbury, 1991

Snitow, Ann, Stansell, Christine and Thompson, Sharon, eds., *The Powers of Desire: The Politics of Sexuality*, New York, Monthly Review/ New Feminist Library, 1983

Stewart, Susan with Persimmon Blackbridge and Lizard Jones, *Drawing the Line: lesbian sexual politics on the wall*, Vancouver, Press Gang Publishers, 1991

Vance, Carole S., ed., *Pleasure and Danger: Exploring Female Sexuality*, Boston, Routledge & Kegan Paul, 1984

Warner, Michael, 'Fear of a Queer Planet', *Social Text*, New York, Vol 9, No 4

Watney, Simon, interview in *frieze*, London, Durian Publications, Issue 2, 1991

Wojnarowicz, David, *Close to the Knives*, New York, Vintage, 1991

Contacts

ACT UP 071 490 5749

Black Gays and Lesbians Against Media Homophobia Freepost, London SE8 5BR

Black HIV/AIDS Network 081 792 9223, 24 hours

Black Lesbian and Gay Helpline 071 837 5364 Thurs 7-10pm

Feminists Against Censorship 38 Mount Pleasant, London WC1

Lesbian and Gay Switchboard 071 837 7324, 24 hours

London Bisexual Group 081 568 1072

London Friend 071 837 3337

London Lesbian Line 071 251 6911

OutRage London Lesbian and Gay Centre, 69 Cowcross Street, London EC1. Telephone: 071 490 7153

Quim BM 2182, London WC1N 3XX. £3.50 (incl p&p)

Shakti for South Asian lesbians and gay men & bisexuals. Women call: 081 802 8981; men call: 081 993 9001

Stonewall 2 Greycoat Place, Westminster, SW1P 1SB

Terrence Higgins Trust 071 242 1010, 3-10pm daily

Out from Scarlet Press

Lesbians Talk Safer Sex
Sue O'Sullivan and Pratibha Parmar

The need for safer sex has revolutionised sexual practice and its discussion within the gay male community and produced a series of hotly contested debates among lesbians which run far deeper than the issue of safer sex itself. Do lesbians need to think about safer sex at all? What has discussion of safer sex revealed about lesbian sexual practices in general? What research has been done on woman-to-woman transmission? Have any of the drugs been tested on women? And are lesbian AIDS activists merely servicing gay men or can we formulate a common agenda? Sue O'Sullivan and Pratibha Parmar discuss the issues. ISBN 1 85727 020 7

Lesbians Talk Issues

Lesbian politics in the 1990s looks set to produce a fast-changing agenda of issues and debates, contradictions and differences of opinion. The **Lesbians Talk Issues** series is designed to provide a forum in which topics of current interest within the international lesbian community can be dissected and discussed with immediacy and flexibility.

*If you would like to write a pamphlet in response to any of the issues raised in **Lesbians Talk Queer Notions** or on any other topical area of lesbian debate, please write to Scarlet Press, 5 Montague Road, London E8 2HN.*